LEGAL GOLD

FOR COACHES

How to Sell and Deliver Coaching,
Training and Consulting
Services to Lawyers

Caroline Newman

LEGAL GOLD FOR COACHES

How to Sell and Deliver Coaching, Training and Consulting Services to Lawyers

First published in 2012 by Ecademy Press

48 St Vincent Drive, St Albans, Herts, AL1 5SJ

info@ecademy-press.com

www.ecademy-press.com

Printed and bound by Lightning Source in the UK and USA. Typeset by Charlotte Mouncey

Printed on acid-free paper from managed forests. This book is printed on demand, so no copies will be remaindered or pulped.

ISBN 978-1-907722-80-6

This book is available online and at all good bookstores.

FOREWORD

This book really is gold. It has everything you need to know about marketing and selling to lawyers and delivering a gold standard service to them. Lawyers understand partnerships. They know how to operate as a firm. Now you will know how to speak their language and create partnerships with them. The book is presented like gold nuggets in a stream, along with some motherlodes, which combine to give you the ultimate handbook to partnering with lawyers to help them be more successful and help yourself in the process. This is the ultimate win-win.

I strongly believe that "Together Everyone Achieves Magic." It's been proven that people benefit from the insights of a good mentor or coach. All top athletes, actors and musicians have a coach. While these people have always had the talent needed to be successful, their coaches, people like you, have helped them realize this talent to get to the top, and stay there. If you are a coach, an expert or consultant, this book will show you how to get your foot in the door of the legal profession. Lawyers need your skills, and are willing to pay you for them. As a highly skilled individual, you can help others improve the way they lead their lives and help them solve their problems.

This book will open doors to you as a coach in a market which is profitable and at the same time very rewarding. Tapping into this market is like opening a restaurant where there are hungry customers who can afford to buy your food. However, you must know how to navigate your way around this market in order to ensure success, and this book is your guide to doing so!

Follow the advice in this book and in a very short time you will have an even more successful business. While you are reading this book, imagine you are on a magic carpet ride. Keep an open mind. Ask yourself empowering questions. Do the exercises and take action.

There are some real insider's secrets that will help you harness your skills and expertise and present them to the legal market using their language.

As you go from the first to last page in this book, you'll have some moments of discovery.

Whatever your goals may be, some things are certain. Once you start taking actions based on the tips in this book you will be able to establish connections with people who are thankful for your skills, and who want you to help them relieve stress and find solutions for a better and more profitable life. You will feel the inner satisfaction that comes from being able to help others, as well as the monetary rewards of a successful career.

So gather your tools and prepare to embark on another successful chapter of your life.

Robert G. Allen

Author of five New York Times best selling books, *One Minute Millionaire, Cash in a Flash, Nothing Down, Creating Wealth* and *Multiple Streams of Income*

ACKNOWLEDGEMENTS

I thank my wonderful children Jelani and Omari for putting up with ready meals and an absent-minded mum for the months it took to put the ideas and thoughts into this book. I love you guys and I'm so proud of you both.

My thanks go to Benn Abdy Collins, Marilyn Devonish, Britney Kara, Liz Adams, Stephen Bailey, Brad Meyer and Dale Burton who gave up their time to review early versions of the manuscript and provide very helpful feedback.

My appreciation goes to Peter Anderson, Partner in the Corporate Department at SJ Berwin LLP for believing in me and taking me under his wings as a new solicitor. Thanks to Remi Bola for his love, support, understand and encouragement whilst I obsessed over how to make this book the best it could be.

I thank Mindy Gibbins-Klein for guidance and unwavering support and for having faith in my ability to deliver this book, and Ecademy Press for publishing this book.

I thank Oprah for being herself and setting the standard for us and Lisa Nichols for her authenticity and inspiration. To Tony Robbins, Bob Proctor, Brian Tracy, Jim Rohn, Jack Canfield, Mark Victor Hansen, Robert G, Allen, Stephen Covey the teachers of the Secret and the original visionaries, coaches and mentors who have walked the walk for many years and paved the way for us to live our dreams of supporting others to live theirs.

My thanks go to Clinton Swaine for making business learning fun and Andy Harrington and the new crop of personal development and business experts that are shining a light for us to follow.

I thank Mike Harris for enabling me to think big and expand my vision of creating and growing an iconic business to fulfill my mission and purpose and my Mastermind Dream Team, Infinity, for encouraging me to multiply my dreams. To Sean Glasgow, my accountability buddy, on this writing and publishing journey, for keeping me focused and believing in me.

Contents

Introduction

About you

I'd like to congratulate you for getting your hands on this book. If you are a coach, trainer or consultant in any niche or specialism and you are looking for more work, then this book is for you. Even though I refer primarily to coaching and coaches throughout this book, all the principles and most of the practices will apply equally to consultants and trainers. In fact, some of the information will be of benefit to anyone who wants to provide services to lawyers.

Why this book? Why now?

I have written this book because many coaches have told me that they find lawyers intimidating. They believe they are smarter than they are. Lawyers have also told me that they find it "frustrating" working with external coaches, trainers and consultants that do not understand them and how they work. The aim of this book is to create a bridge for you to meet lawyers where they are.

If you are experiencing these issues below then this is the right book for you, right now. If you care passionately about helping people and you have a product or service that can genuinely help lawyers to solve some of the problems they have, then I welcome you.

Do you want to:

- Access the legal market (and have not been able to do so?)

- Establish a more stable income?

- Build a better network to earn referrals without the

tedious breakfast meetings, and cozy conversations that lead nowhere?

- Grow your business or practice with new referrals?

- Learn how to sell and improve your conversion rates?

Are you:

- Eager to attract more leads from law firms, but can't figure out where to find those leads or how to attract them into your business?

- Looking for more clients that are more profitable to your business?

- Frustrated that your business is stuck in one place and isn't going forward?

- Under pressure to improve your Return On Investment (ROI) from networking?

- Scared that if you don't start networking more effectively, you're going to lose your business?

- Trying to break in to the legal business, or just trying to learn more about it?

Have you:

- Had a negative experience working with a lawyer?

Then this book will help you.

Why the "Gold Mine" Metaphor?

You may be wondering why I think that the legal business is like a gold mine for coaches, consultants and trainers throughout the world at this time. Well, when the gold rush first begun in the spring of 1849, the first people who were able to excavate and benefit from the gold were the ones who were first and prepared to dig deep for gold. This is what you have to do these days to get your hands full of good quality clients in our profession. It occurred to me that there are little nuggets of information that I can share with you. There are nuggets out there, the "low hanging fruit", and there is potential to find a motherlode. I show you how to avoid the grit and go for legal gold.

Latest, Cutting Edge Information

In this book you will find up to date information, tips and suggestions that will help you. It is said that people will do anything for those who encourage their dreams; justify their failures; allay their fears; confirm their suspicions and help them throw rocks at their enemies. Well lawyers are no different! This book is relevant for your business now. The legal profession is going through very radical and unprecedented changes. Some lawyers realize that in order to overcome and survive in this new legal market place they will have to change the way they do things.

Lawyers' Current Problems

"The first thing we do, let's kill all the lawyers". This quote from Henry VI (part 2) is often misquoted against legal practitioners. But Shakespeare puts these words into the mouth of Dick the butler the revolutionary, to underline that the rule of law is a bulwark for a stable and civilized society.

My outcome is to "skill" lawyers instead of killing them. Unlike Dick the butler, the revolution we are proposing is not to overthrow democracy! But it is my sincere desire to assist lawyers in finding and applying the skills that will make them even better lawyers. You can help them to deal with the business, health and emotional problems that they have.

All is not well in the legal profession. The Bar is doing alright - in so far as it continues to be a great life for the handful at the top end, as it has always been - but things are pretty uncertain for almost everybody else. The real angst is being felt among the ranks of the middle-sized firms of solicitors.

As of 6th October 2011, in the UK, the legal market has been opened up to non lawyers. In the past lawyers had to organize themselves as partnerships with only other lawyers. For the first time, businesses other than solicitors are allowed to offer a range of legal services. Now anyone can set up a limited company and provide legal services. This is the long-heralded opening up of the legal market to outside competition.

Companies such as Tesco (Wal-Mart equivalent in the US) can now provide legal services. This is being called "Tesco law". This means that they are muscling into the legal market. They can provide services that used to be the exclusive preserve of lawyers now. In the US discussions about de-regulation of legal services are also taking place.

This means that the profession is in a state of flux. Lawyers are struggling. Some will survive. Some will need to leave the profession and possibly retrain to do something else. Big firms may be floating on the stock markets for the first time. Some may be merging. Medium sized firms will have little option but to merge. They will require assistance to do this and manage the change and help their employees to manage the change. Unfortunately for lawyers, one of the obvious areas Tesco have targeted is conveyancing. This is the legal work surrounding the buying and selling of houses and apartments. This is for the twin reasons that the work is frequently straightforward, usually does not require a sophisticated, legal knowledge, and is regularly high margin. The problem is that a large proportion of solicitors' income comes from this and divorce.

The other problem - although it affects specialists rather than the mainstream -is the cuts to legal aid and the curbs on "no win, no fee" litigation. Again, for some, these were major sources of income.

Life was already tough for these firms because of the economic slowdown which started around 2008. They are in no condition to withstand further loss of income. Consequently the industry is bracing itself for a shake out. Some may be able to survive by merging if it allows them to retain the revenues of both firms but live as cheaply as one by cutting back office costs and overheads. But many others don't really have much to offer a merger partner. For them, the outlook is bleak. Many will just have to accept that they will be earning less.

Big Firms, for example have problems attracting and developing the best people, executive development; employee engagement; attracting and keeping clients; maintaining their energy.

One of the definitions of a professional is that they have to belong to a professional body which has rules (in the case of solicitors their rules are enshrined in law and also significant) and amongst other things is a person whose professional status requires them to behave in ways which are often against their own commercial (or industrial) interests. The word profession suggests privilege and the ability to charge highly for a service. They believe they are under threat and that the current government is doing its best to undermine their status. They believe that they are not as highly regarded (or paid) as doctors - presumably because the public do not value their services. They are asking how they can to re-establish themselves as a valued profession - without either clinging to the past or becoming super efficient machines.

They find it difficult to understand the thinking from some sources that behaving as professionals is akin to being dinosaurs without value or merit, whilst behaving as though they are an industry is lauded as a sign of progress and merit.

Professional values and ethics do not become outmoded simply because they have existed for a long time. However much politicians and consumer groups do not like to admit it, there remains a fundamental difference in law between a "client" and a "customer", not least the requirement to always act in the best interests of the former.

Some lawyers find it difficult to cope with the prospect of supermarkets providing legal services. They don't believe that supermarkets always think of their customers first. They believe that the market themselves on the premise of convincing their customers they are giving them what they want - and that however, is not necessarily what is in the best interests of those clients.

The belief is that the law and the legal system cannot always deliver what the "customer" wants. Sometimes what they want what is legally impossible or extremely unlikely to occur. They wonder whether supermarkets will give advice as "professionals" even though it is not what they want to hear. Or should they behave as an industry and try to sell them something else in the hope they can convince them they need it?

The recent report from the UK Legal Services Board states that it is their duty to promote competition within the legal services market and that alternative business structures are going to happen whether lawyers like it or not. The "Market Consolidators" (Tesco) are seen as a threat to the traditional High Street practice because they are investing in technology to drive down acquisition and document production costs, they are employing lower cost paralegals (including law graduates who cannot find a training contract) rather than taking on trainees or Newly Qualified staff, and they are bundling services to cross sell more effectively.

The Bar has not escaped these problems. Most of their work comes from Solicitors, who may have less work and what they have they may want to keep "in house" instead of giving it to barristers. Recently, for the first time Barristers are able to provide their services directly to the public. This means that they have to operate as a traditional business. As most of them are not trained to do this, they will need your help to grow their business.

The message is very clear lawyers must adapt or die. I believe that to succeed in the future, firms and individual lawyers will need to: -

1. Differentiate themselves, get a 'brand';

2. Become fantastic at customer service and probably innovative in this respect too;

3. Embrace social media in order to build 1) and publicize 2); and

4. Use technology to become faster and more efficient - i.e. work smarter, not harder/longer to deliver a sensibly priced service (I am not suggesting competing on price) but essentially becoming more profitable by spending less time on repetitive/non-legal/non-specialist task that clients do not want to, nor should have to pay a premium for.

Why I know you can help

I am passionate about coaching. Over the years I have had many coaches for the different areas of my business and my life. But this is about you! If you're a coach, trainer and consultant then the chances are, like me, you have been exposed to the best business mentors and coaches. We have been so fortunate to be taught by the founders of the coaching profession, Tony Robbins, Brian Tracy, Bob Proctor, Jim Rohn, Stephen Covey, the teachers on "The Secret" and other remarkable mentors. There is now a new group of dynamic, innovative coaches who want to professionalize the business and ensure its ongoing development and improvement.

When I worked in law firms I knew nothing about these matters. Neither did most of my colleagues. Lawyers in big firms go to work in the morning and are usually in the office all day, drafting contracts, in client meetings, at court or managing the business. Many are not happy. Some of them feel like they are in a "sausage machine". They feel unappreciated and undervalued. They need your insight, your objectivity, your passion and your gift. So whatever your particular niche you can expand into the legal market. So prepare yourself today for this opportunity to diversify your income.

Golddiggers not welcome!

The main message of this book is for coaches to learn how lawyers are trained, how they work, what problems they face and how you can market your services to lawyers. And, how if you can learn to modify your business plan using all the suggestions in this book, then you will be well on your way to finding your "golden clients" However, the essence of the book is about Partnership. Please think win-win. If you approach this voyage with that attitude, you will be welcomed, appreciated and valued.

Human Resources in Law Firms

I hope that people in Human Resources in law firms and chambers read this book. This book will give you an insight into the problems faced by lawyers and how you as one of the potential purchasers of the services can find out what is available to help your people do their jobs better at work, consistently reach their targets and be happier.

Some of you have told me over the years how frustrated you are that the people who are selling to you, training, coaching and providing other services to you, do not understand how lawyers work, what problems they face, or what rules they need to follow at all times. This book will help you make the choices about who can help you to help your people be the best they can be. There will be a small army of well informed and trained coaches ready to help you and your bosses solve your problems consistently and professionally.

Non UK lawyers

Lawyers from other jurisdictions will have a better understanding the UK legal system. Over the years, I have been surprised to learn that many US attorneys do not understand the difference between a solicitor and a barrister! While the legal system of every country around the world varies at least somewhat, I think it is helpful that lawyers understand the basics of the legal system in each country. We are living in a truly global time. There are many international law firms and law has no borders. Most lawyers are passionate about justice and the rule of law, wherever they may be.

Law Students

I also hope that this book will offer insight to students who want to become lawyers. When I was studying, I had no idea what was really going on in law firms. Why would I? You are more fortunate. Even if you are lucky enough to have a good career advice team they won't know most of the information in this book. If you have a training contract, pupillage or another training arrangement, congratulations! You are one of the lucky ones. You will now be aware of the resources available to help you make the transition from student to employee. You have the right to ask your HR team to give you all the support you need to succeed. This book will inform and empower you to ask for the support.

If you don't yet have a training arrangement in place, then you have my empathy. Research conducted in August 2011 (produced in the London Metro) shows that 54.7% of law students in the UK will never get a training contract to qualify as a solicitor. The statistics are just as grim in Canada, Australia and the US. If you are truly determined to qualify into the profession in these difficult times you will need help over and above what you career advisor can give you. If you are a student and you have bought or been given this book then I am pleased for you. The information here will help you to increase your odds of qualifying in the legal profession.

You will learn things that they do not teach you in college. If you apply the information in this book you will improve your chances of qualifying and succeeding in your chosen profession. This information will help you to get your foot in the door so you too can have access to the gold that is available, and always will be, in spite of the current challenges, in the provision of legal services. Lawyers are very good at ensuring their own survival! They have friends in very high places and, in my observation; these vested interests will always find a way to survive.

Lawyer problems

Lawyers have the usual problems that small business owners have with attracting and keeping good clients; attracting and retaining the best staff; time management; leadership and management; sales and business development and work life balance. Throughout the book I have listed some of the specific problems that you can help lawyers to deal with.

Take Action

As a coach, I believe that people should take action. At the end of each chapter you will be invited to take action to implement what you have read. Why not set some goals for what you want to achieve in reading this book and take action whilst you read.

Lawyer Jokes

Because I am constantly told that coaches find lawyers intimidating I have included some howlers delivered by lawyers around the globe. These quotes are from a variety of sources. Some are from a book called "Disorder in The American Courts," and are things people actually said in court, word for word, taken down and now published by court reporters who had the torment of staying calm while these exchanges were actually taking place. Others have been emailed to me over the years by colleagues. I hope you enjoy them and have a laugh!

Have a laugh

Lawyer: "Do you recall the time that you examined the body?"
Witness: "The autopsy started around 8:30 p.m."
Lawyer: "And Mr. Dennington was dead at the time?"
Witness: "No, he was sitting on the table wondering why I was doing an autopsy."

and another…

Lawyer: "What is your date of birth?"
Witness: "July 15th".
Lawyer: "What year?"
Witness: "Every year."

and another…

Lawyer: " Are you sexually active?"
Witness: "No, I just lie there."

and another…

Lawyer: "What gear were you in at the moment of the impact?"
Witness: "Gucci sweats and Reeboks."

and another…

Lawyer: "How old is your son, the one living with you?

Witness: "Thirty-eight or thirty-five, I can't remember which."

Lawyer: "How long has he lived with you?"

Witness: "Forty-five years."

Good Luck and Best Wishes

Caroline Newman

London 2012

Help me if you can

- Publicize myself effectively
- Promote myself
- Create a media presence
- Create a buzz around myself
- What to say and who to say it to
- Manage press releases
- Create a positive media image

SECTION I -
Who's Who In The Legal Professions

When the miners started to look for gold in the streams and mines, they weren't sure how much exactly they were looking for. Some were happy just to find a few nuggets of gold, while others strived to look for the motherlode - a major artery of gold.

This section will teach you the different ways that gold will be available to you in the legal mine. You can either spend time drilling for the motherlode and land a large contract with a big firm or you can pan for the nuggets among the individual lawyers, attorneys, barristers or small practice owner.

Mining is a still a complicated matter with many potential pitfalls. Learning how to mine requires first a desire to do whatever it takes. So, be like the "49ers" as the early gold miners were called, get prepared to dig as deep as you need to go to find the gold. However, you are in luck, because as you will see mining in the 21st Century is a very different ball game. These days, thanks to modern technology you don't need a lot of expensive equipment, but, it does require a desire to learn the tricks of the trade from successful miners. You can choose to work a single claim, locally, nationally, or internationally; expanding your mining operations into firms around the world.

Chapter 1 - Big Wigs

In the UK, judges and barristers wear wigs in court, hence the chapter title. I'm told they are very uncomfortable to wear and can advance baldness! The big wigs in the legal business are judges in the higher courts and Queen's Counsels (QCs). The UK's judiciary is composed of 7 main groups of judges with each group performing slightly different duties at different levels of the legal business. That said, essentially their duty remains the same; they preside over hearings and make judgments on the cases presented before them.

1. Lord Chief Justices

2. High Court Judges

3. Circuit Judges

4. Recorders, Masters and Registrars

5. District Judges

6. Deputy District Judges

7. Magistrates

Magistrates are also judges; they only preside over minor cases that are presented in Magistrate's Court. The typical process is as follows: three magistrates present at any hearing with the lead magistrate being a qualified legal professional. The other two are lay magistrates who are picked from very diverse walks of life to ensure that cases are dealt with fairly and that there is no bias in the decisions. The lead magistrate will review the list of cases to be presented before the court to ensure that the magistrates do not know any of the people involved in the cases.

Judges and magistrates perform slightly different duties; however both are very influential on the legal system. Magistrates are responsible for dealing with minor cases (which constitute the majority of court appearances) and the majority of these cases will be tried in Magistrate's Court, unless they are passed to higher courts, where judges preside over more serious cases.

The occupation of a judge or magistrate is a very difficult and stressful one. I have been coaching them for a while and you can too. While judges receive the relevant professional training from the Judicial Studies Board, they will buy coaching to help them deal with the immense pressures placed on them. They sometimes face the dilemma of dealing with the difference in the quality of representation; for example when an individual chooses to represent themselves but faces a highly skilled lawyer who is working for a corporation.

Judges are considered the big wigs in the legal profession because not only do they have the most power, they also have a lot of influence over their colleagues, and other lawyers. They make a lot of money, usually in the 6 figures or at least very high 5 figures, which means they have the resources to invest in their own personal improvement by enlisting the services of a coach or consultant.

In my personal experience that I have amassed as a coach, judges often just want someone to talk to. They want someone to listen to them, discuss their values, help them set goals, review targets, help them practice time management, help them manage stress and other health issues. Sometimes, they need someone to help them walk through why they made a particular decision, especially if they are feeling doubtful about the decision or the circumstances that led to it.

How Lawyers Become Judges

In England and Wales, in the lower courts, the positions are advertised in the legal press and on the Judicial Appointments Commission website. Lawyers complete a comprehensive application form. They are required to demonstrate competency in five key areas. Then for most posts they are invited to take a written test. Then most will be asked to take place in a role play where they play the judge. This is followed by a 45 minute panel interview. Competition for these posts is intense, especially in the current market. Lawyers see a judicial post, part-time or full time as providing a degree of security and possible progression to a full time position as a judge in one of the Higher Courts.

As you become a more experienced at coaching lawyers you might also become a specialist in coaching judges and Queens Counsel.

Have a laugh

Lawyer: "This myasthenia gravis, does it affect your memory at all?"
Witness: "Yes."
Lawyer: "And in what ways does it affect your memory?"
Witness: "I forget."
Lawyer: "You forget? Can you give us an example of something that you've forgotten?"

and another...

Judge: "Now, as we begin, I must ask you to banish all present information and prejudice from your minds, if you have any."

Help me with these

- Understand and handle Trainees and Pupils better

- Manage my employees

- Evaluate my staff fairly

- Conduct competency based assessments

- Delegate to others successfully

- Introduce and manage change

Now do something!
Knowledge is potential power.
Action is real power!

What 3 actions could you take right now?

1. _____

_____

_____

2. _____

_____

_____

3. _____

_____

_____

Chapter 2 - Little Wigs

I refer to barristers as the 'little wigs' in the legal business. Some barristers earn more than a High Court Judge. In the past, barristers and solicitors were exclusive occupations - barristers had the right to work in higher courts, while solicitors were limited to lower courts. That has now changed and solicitors can train to become Solicitor Advocates.

England and Wales have mostly broken down the barriers between barristers and solicitors, some countries still maintain the professional distance between the two occupations.

A barrister is a member of one of the two classes of lawyer found in many common law jurisdictions with split legal professions. Barristers specialize in courtroom advocacy, drafting legal pleadings and giving expert legal opinions.

It used to be the case that without a solicitor appointing a barrister to represent their client, a barrister may not represent a client. This changed in 2009 when Barristers, in restricted areas of law, were allowed to have direct access to the client.

Barristers' Legal Education and Training

To qualify as a barrister a person must complete a 3-year law degree followed by a one year Bar Professional Training Course (BPTC). A smaller number qualify having completed a non-law degree, followed by a one year law conversion course. They then study for one year to pass the BPSC. They are now able to call themselves barristers.

Training

Newly qualified barristers who want to appear in court are required to do a 12 month training program with a set of chambers. Chambers is a place where groups of barristers work. It is operated as a collective. All barristers in chambers are self employed. They are looked after by clerks, who promote them to solicitors, manage their diaries and the day to day administration and management of the chambers. The clerks are managed by a senior clerk. Most chambers in London are in the Temple, Lincolns Inn, Holborn, and Grays Inn.

Barristers and solicitors receive their roles by completing relevant law education and formal training process. Like most professionals, they receive no formal training on leadership management, supervision or marketing their skills. Most importantly, they are also averse to the concept of selling their skills, which can prevent their business from becoming as profitable as it could be.

A coach or consultant could help barristers and solicitors work through problems like: learning how to market their business; how to create an online presence for themselves or their firm; how to ensure that clients are satisfied with their services.

Coaches or consultants may also have to help barristers and solicitors deal with the stress and personal problems that arrise from being a part of the legal business - politicians, lawyers, victims, the accused, the plaintiff and the defendant, problems in chambers/law firms, to name but a few.

Being a lawyer is incredibly time consuming to work on even one case. A lawyer's role consists of preparing evidence, collecting and reading statements, crafting court arguments, the legwork of researching their clients, their situation, carrying the constant stress of wondering whether they will win for their client. As such coaching requires a strong up front agreement.

Barriers to entry

There are no barriers to entry for you as the coach. Once you have built up your reputation, chambers and law firms will call on you to coach their barristers and solicitors. Also you will benefit from word of mouth referrals.

Of course like most people lawyers may not be ready to face up to the major issues in their lives and may make excuses. However, if the barrister has an emotional issue it can be amplified because of the immense responsibly of the role.

Have a laugh

Lawyer: "Now doctor, isn't it true that when a person dies in his sleep, he doesn't know about it until the next morning?"

Witness: "Did you actually pass the bar exam?"

Help me with these

- Build a cohesive Team

- Create a dream team

- Pick the right candidates as trainees

- Get my team to co-operate

- Develop team building exercises

- Provide developmental resources to my staff

Now do something!
Knowledge is potential power.
Action is real power!

What 3 actions could you take right now?

1. _____

   _____

   _____

2. _____

   _____

   _____

3. _____

   _____

   _____

Chapter 3 - No Wigs

No wigs are solicitors, attorneys, paralegals, legal executives, trainee solicitors. Just because they don't wear wigs! While the legal executives and trainee solicitors in firms don't have very much influence on the structure of the legal world, they may still require the services of coaches and consultants. Some legal executives feel that they are not as valued as solicitors, even though they do essentially the same work.

Number of solicitors

The number of law firms in England and Wales has continued its inexorable rise, with 25% more in practice than a decade before. The Law Society's annual statistical report also shows the impact of the recession on the largest City practices, which employed 5% fewersolicitors in 2010 than two years previously - despite a 4% rise in solicitors working in private practice overall - with partner numbers taking a particular hit.

The report - which reflects the state of the profession as at 31 July 2010 - said there were 10,413 private practice law firms on that date, a slight increase on 2009. There were just 8,319 firms operating in 2000, although growth slowed in the second part of the decade.

It had been thought a few years ago that there were even more firms, but changes in data collection reduced the number. As a result the report's authors say examining trends should be treated with "some caution".

There were 20,318 practicing solicitors working in the largest law firms (81 partners or more) in 2010 - 23% of all solicitors in private practice. This compares to 21,322 in 2008, when they comprised 26% of all solicitors. The number of partners fell 7% to 5,917.

The disparity between men and women in terms of partnership - exposed by previous editions of the report - shows little sign of improving. Some 48% of male private practice solicitors are partners, compared to 21% of females.

Though some of this is because there are more senior men in the profession than women, the report said: "Even after equalizing the levels of experience, higher proportions of men achieved partnership status than women. In all of the experience bands, a lower proportion of women than men were partners or sole practitioners. Of solicitors in private practice with 10-19 years' experience - the band with the greatest number of partners and sole practitioners - 72.4% of men were partners or sole practitioners, compared to only 44.6% women."

Overall, there were 150,128 solicitors on the solicitors roll, 53% of whom were male, and 117,862 with practicing certificates (54% male). Around 13% of solicitors with a known ethnicity came from minority ethnic (BME) groups.

The number of practicing solicitors has more than tripled in just 30 years - there were 37,832 in 1980.

The report also illustrates the amazing growth in law as a subject for study - 19,000 applied for law at university in 1999, compared to more than 29,000 a decade later. The number accepted onto courses grew from 11,154 to almost 20,000 in the same period; almost a third of them are now from BME backgrounds.

However, after a fall of 19% in the number of students who then enrolled with the Law Society to study on the legal practice course between 2008 and 2009, to 8,098, the figure is back to virtually the same level it was a decade earlier - although there has been a massive increase in the number of full and part-time places on the LPC during that time, from 8,876 to 15,166. The number of training contracts fell 16% in 2009/10, to 4,874, the lowest level since 1998/99

Legal Executives

Legal executives are trained legal professionals in England & Wales. They usually specialize in a particular area of law, usually residential & commercial conveyance, wills & trusts, personal injury, family law, criminal law, employment law, immigration law and litigation. They join the Institute of Legal Executives and thereafter complete the required education and practical experience that is needed for them to perform some of the duties of a solicitor. (However, it must be noted, that in many places abroad, their legal equivalents are usually considered to have a lower professional status.)

Trainee solicitors

Trainee solicitors are in training to qualify. These trainees may also need a coach or a mentor so that they can get through their training and maintain their sanity. They then need to plan to execute their rise to the top of the profession while navigating the internal politics, competitive nature of the profession, long hours, poor management and supervision and isolation.

In house lawyers

There is an army of lawyers (barristers, solicitors and attorneys) employed within corporations, government and local government. These companies have huge training budgets.

Coaching Solicitors and others

Contrary to what is projected on TV and in the movies, some solicitors and attorneys have issues around confidence, self esteem, goal setting and time management. Trainees in big firms get access to a variety of training, the quality of which is variable. If you can create an innovative program that meets the need you will be welcomed with open arms. Find out where the trainee events are being held. In the UK you can Google "Trainee solicitors" and you will find their website. Firms will normally pay for good quality training for their trainees. But if they are struggling and don't want the firm to know they may approach you directly in confidence. In this case either they, or their parents, will pay you.

How many lawyers are there?

Number of Law firms in England and Wales - 10,500 (2010)

Solicitors in England and Wales - 150,000 (120,000 of these have practicing certificates/ licenses)

Barristers - 12,500 (a further 3000 are employed in companies or law firms) (2010)

US Attorneys - 1.2 million (2010)

Australian lawyers 99,000

Canadian Lawyers 68,000

Trainees - Around 10,000 (both first and second year trainees combined) 2010

Legal Executives in England and Wales 22,000

I regard a "big firm" as the top 200 law firms in London and the Regions. In the US you can easily find out who the biggest firms are and where to find them!

The Structure of Law Firms

Up until 5th October 2011, law firms were owned exclusively by lawyers and were managed by the Partners. In big firms they are assisted by a Chief Executive Officer (CEO) and a board which includes the usual posts. In some firms the CEO and Partners have a difficult working relationship, because they approach problems from different perspectives and possibly consider different solutions to be appropriate.

A coach or consultant could help these people get past their problems and to the top of their part of the legal business. A coach or mentor can help each of these professionals with many things.

You can assist legal executives and paralegals to build a professional image for themselves in their target market, as well as help them discover how to improve themselves.

Trainee solicitors: help to discover which area of law they want to go into, and how to succeed in that particular area.

CEOs and Partners: help can include building understanding of each other's difficulties as well as help to work through the stress that they face as they continuously compete in a rapidly evolving market. They need ideas and assistance to eliminate waste, cut costs, manage stress and make difficult decisions.

Team Selection

Even as a junior lawyer I remember being puzzled at the method used by some lawyers to select teams. Often a Partner would be given a new deal or project. It appeared that often the most important criteria for selection of the team seemed to be who had "capacity" (this means those lawyers who had little or no work).

There was no profiling, role analysis, interview or assessment to determine the best way to put the team together. As you can imagine often the team would disintegrate or the professional jealousies (to which I refer) could jaundice the team.

Internal Politics

It can get quite territorial between the different departments in the firm. For example, I have witnessed near warfare within a team which was set up to deliver a client's project. Some of the lawyers refuse to cross refer, even in the same firm. They are driven by a fear that "their" client will build a better relationship with someone else in the firm and they will lose the status as the "Client Partner".

Have a laugh

Lawyer: "Do you know if your daughter has ever been involved in voodoo or the occult?"

Witness: "We both do."

Lawyer: "Voodoo?"

Witness: "We do."

Lawyer: "You do?"

Witness: "Yes, voodoo."

Help me with these problems

- Work with my seniors to move forward the corporate plan

- Create transparency between the higher and lower levels of my staff

- Develop the art of diplomacy

- Deal with bullying and harassment

- Work with my partners and my CEO

- Hold productive meetings

Now do something!
Knowledge is potential power.
Action is real power!

What 3 actions could you take right now?

1. _____

   _____

   _____

2. _____

   _____

   _____

3. _____

   _____

   _____

Chapter 4 - Lawyers Around the World

As a result of my activity on social media sites I now have friends from nearly every country in the world, perhaps you do too. This is just a taster about the different jurisdictions. There are some experiences that are global and some local. If you want to target lawyers in these countries then you can get more information on Google. The internet and social media means that your coaching practice can truly be international.

European Lawyers

This section considers the position of lawyers from other member states of the European Union. It does not go into detail about the different legal systems but, provides a broad outline of the hoops these lawyers have to go through if they want to qualify in the UK. Consultants and coaches can assist them with this transition. There are transition coaches who specialize in assisting newcomers to the country.

Scotland

Scotland's legal system is separate from those of England and Wales and Northern Ireland. In Scotland, the legal profession is divided between solicitors and advocates, the distinction being similar to that between solicitors and barristers in England and Wales, In Scotland, solicitors are regulated by the Scottish Law society. All solicitors in Scotland are required to complete 20 hours of continuing professional development each year. Local law societies lobby on behalf of their members with The Law Society of Scotland and The Scottish Government regarding future legal developments. You can coach lawyers in Scotland.

Australia

Regulation of the profession in Australia varies from state to state. Admission to practice is state-based, although mutual recognition enables a practitioner admitted in any state to practice nationally. In some states, the distinction between barristers and solicitors is nominal and reflects individual preferences and membership of professional associations. In others, at least in a practical sense, the distinction is clear from the type of practice practitioners have, even if they are entitled to practice in the other branch of the profession. Thus, while members of the bar practice only as barristers, a practitioner is admitted as a "barrister and solicitor." Thus, every solicitor is also a barrister, although many prefer to brief counsel rather than appear in courts or tribunals themselves. The trend to a fused profession is similar to that outlined above in England and Wales.

The states of New South Wales and Queensland, however, maintain strongly independent bars, call to which requires extra training. In those states, solicitors' rights of audience before superior courts are theoretically unlimited, but infrequently exercised in practice. Victoria also has an independent bar but solicitors have full right of audience before all courts. You can coach lawyers in Australia.

At the end of June 2008, the Australian legal services sector employed 99,696 people.

In all, there were 15,326 businesses and organizations engaged in providing legal services or legal support services. Of the 99,696 people employed by the Australian legal services sector at the end of June 2008:

- 5,154 (5.2 per cent) were either barristers or employed by barristers;

- 5,108 (5.1 per cent) were employed in community legal services, including legal aid commissions, Aboriginal legal services and community legal centers;

- 4,514 (4.5 per cent) worked in the offices of government solicitors or public prosecutors; and

- 84,921 (85.2 per cent) worked in "other" legal services including private law firms

Contribution to the Economy

The Australian legal services sector generated income of $18b during the 2007-08 financial year and contributed $10.9b to the Australian economy.

Other Legal Services

At the end of June 2008, there were 11,244 "other" legal services businesses, which employed 84,921 people. These businesses comprised solicitor firms, patent attorney businesses, service/payroll entities and other businesses providing various legal support services.

Of these businesses, the vast majority (78.2 per cent or 8,795) were located in capital cities. These capital city businesses accounted for 81 per cent (or 68,828) of all people employed in other legal services and generated 87.6 per cent (or $12.9b) of the income. Other legal services earned the majority of their income from commercial law (33.6 per cent) and property

Canada - In the English-speaking common law jurisdictions of Canada, the professions of barrister and solicitor have been fused; all lawyers are called to the bar and admitted as solicitors. While many barristers and solicitors choose to practice within the scope of one or the other traditional disciplines, many others choose a cross-discipline practice. In Quebec, however, like America and modern France, there is no tradition of split professions, though a distinction is sometimes made between an "avocat plaidant" - trial lawyer and an "avocat-conseil" or "conseiller juridique" - legal consultant. There are 68,000 lawyers in Canada.

United States

In the US lawyers are called attorneys. The title is an amalgamation of the roles. Attorneys are appointed by the different state bars in the 50 States. You can find out more by searching the websites of the State Bar Associations. There are many groups, Bar Associations statewide as well as the American Bar Association. US judges are appointed by the Senate & the President. There are around 1.2 million attorneys in the US.

How lawyers get paid

Judges

Judges are on a salary. They are essentially government employees. Most of them earn six figures. Part time judges are also full time practicing barristers or solicitors. They will be paid a daily rate. They are required to work a minimum period, around 8 weeks to maintain their positions. They will continue to get income from their practices.

Barristers

A barrister's income will vary massively depending on their area of practice. Newly- qualified barristers are on a low salary. The most senior barristers can earn up to one million pounds a year. Senior QCs in the commercial sectors can command income above that sum. The income of many barristers who do mainly legal aid work also varies. Some will not be earning a great deal. Some of them, by the time you calculate the number of hours they work could even be on minimum wage. You can find out how senior a barrister is by looking at their profile on their website or their chamber's website. It will have a date when they are "called". This is the date they were formally enrolled as barristers. Barristers pay rent for their rooms in chambers and they have to contribute an agreed percentage of their income towards chambers administration and maintenance.

Attorneys and solicitors

These lawyers are on salaries plus bonuses. Generally the more senior a lawyer is the more they get paid. Also the more specialist they are the more they get paid. City lawyers get paid a lot more than others and bigger bonuses! You can find out how long a solicitor has been qualified by looking at the Law Society's website which contains a list of all solicitors.

Sole practitioners essentially exchange their time for money and earn whatever they can. They are essentially small business owners. They might need to consider discontinuing as generalists as they cannot compete with Tesco on price or service. They may need help to become specialist in their field, to build effective online presence, outsource non essentials, get the best insurance and focus on being of service in a niche market in their local area.

Partners in law firms

The new or junior partners will be on a salary plus bonuses until they buy into the partnership and become equity partners. Partners in the top city firms can earn over $1.5 million a year.

Don't forget the amazing support staff

As well as lawyers there is an army the other professions in the big law firms, including marketing, IT, information and knowledge management, accounts, post room staff, secretaries. Having an understanding of the law firm will also open up possibilities for you there also.

Have a laugh

Lawyer: "What was the first thing your husband said to you when he woke up that morning?"

Witness: "He said, "Where am I, Cathy?""

Lawyer: "And why did that upset you?"

Witness: " My name is Susan".

Help me if you can

- How do we attract and retain a diverse workforce?

- How we honor our legal obligations?

- How do we manage diversity?

- How do we understand and deliver on diversity according to our Code of Practice?

- Our clients and staff are now international. How do we understand different cultures?

- What policies do we need and how do we get the right policies in place?

- How do we handle disputes before they get out of control and damage our reputation?

Now do something!
Knowledge is potential power.
Action is real power!

What 3 actions could you take right now?

1. _____

_____

_____

2. _____

_____

_____

3. _____

_____

_____

SECTION II -
How You Can Help

When the 49ers heard that there was gold in a particular location they picked up their tools and went to mine there. They heard the stories of the few people who had discovered motherlodes. So everyone thought that they could be the next one to hit a motherlode. There is a market in helping lawyers to be more successful. But you need to do some work first and you need to be aware of the timewasters out there. There are people who will try to get you to give them advice, without paying for it.

I've decided that there is no competition only creation. There is plenty for everyone. The majority of the people who were a part of the 1849 gold rush ended up having nothing to their name.

Chapter 5 - The Problem with Lawyers

It seems that since the dawn of time, lawyers have been getting bad press. They are regarded as "ambulance chasers", masters of trickery, and word twisters. People tell me that they are scared that if they talk to lawyers, their words will be molded into something that shows them in a bad light. People feel that lawyers overcharge for their services, in an attempt to rip them off and make tons of profit themselves.

If we look at these things from a lawyer's point of view you will find that lawyers are people just like you. To be effective at their jobs, lawyers need to be able to pick the slightest loophole in words, and be able to use it to their client's advantage; this does not mean that they are out to trick you, but in fact it means that they are better able to protect their clients ; from bad contracts, ineffective laws etc. As for the costs, a lot of money is invested in a lawyer, and they must make that up somehow. It costs £200,000 to train a solicitor, along with all the university fees, and law school fees that lawyers have to pay even before they can be trained.

Lawyers such as Gandhi have played an essential role in the fabric of society for a very long time. Many former British Prime Ministers and Parliament members were lawyers before they went into politics. As were many former Presidents of the

United States. Because lawyers are so necessary for the effective operating of our society, and our justice system, it is necessary that lawyers aren't stalled by their personal and profession problems and that the legal business isn't stuck in a rut. This is where good coaches are always of service.

The legal business is changing so rapidly, becoming increasingly competitive and problematic that legal firms are struggling to make a profit due to these changes in the marketplace. Whilst lawyers are technically skilled they lack the necessary skills required for the next phase of their business (chambers) and the development of a well-designed business system, without problems.

Lawyers are not trained in people skills nor how to market their services and how to make themselves attractive to their clients; problem solving, or accessing creativity. They are under threat from competitors, i.e. large companies and banks. Research conducted by the British Law Society demonstrated that the main problem facing legal firm associates is that managers do not know how to manage, develop or supervise their employees. As it costs £200,000 to train a solicitor it is a huge loss to any law firm if a solicitor chooses to leave due to stress not related to legal matters

A lawyer who wants to set up their own firm often has little or no business skills, especially in brand management, promotion, marketing and sales.

We are not in the most financially stable times right now. There is competitiveness in every area of the market, especially in the legal services market. And, this is particularly challenging for lawyers because most of them aren't trained to be business people. How do they deal with price competition when someone else will offer the same services that they do at a quarter of their rate?

In turn, lawyers turn to "efficient" business strategies by adopting cost-cutting that in turn negatively impact their business future. Client care, an imperative factor in getting the customer to choose them, is detracted from. The amount of professionals working for the business is cut with most "efficient" businesses hiring very few barristers, few solicitors, some legal executives, but mostly untrained semi-professionals! The experience and skill required to provide for the client is cut to the bone and ultimately service and performance suffer.

According to the laws of marketing: the only way you can convince your customer that you deserve to be paid four times the competition (see above) is to completely stand out from the crowd. And, that is where coaches can excel at bolstering the ability of lawyers to run their businesses by enabling them to build their business, brand and service strategies.

You can help lawyers to set themselves apart from the crowd and ensure their clients that they are the best option available. Your goal as a coach is to help lawyers develop REAL efficient businesses so that they can earn a profit without having to completely destroy the validity of the legal business.

Dealing with the Problem of Selling

Lawyers simply do not like to. They know that they have to do it to survive. The reasons why lawyers think that they shouldn't or couldn't sell their services include: lack of time; believing that they're above selling their services; believing that selling is "dirty"; believing that lawyers should only handle law and leave the rest to someone else.

But lawyers can no longer afford to be shy or snobbish. They have to put their service out there, make it stand out from the crowd and be prepared to deal with interested prospects. This is the only way that they can attract clients in this type of economy.

While times may be tough now, they're going to get tougher. Competition increases every moment, and if they don't know how to attract clients then there's no chance of them succeeding. Lawyers will have to start behaving as an industry, and stop hiding behind the façade of a profession.

About the Legal Profession, Service Providers and Marketing

Some lawyers tell me that they are frustrated with coaches, consultants and trainers who do not understand how they operate and how their businesses are structured. As a result they are left with a negative impression.

Lawyers especially have a problem with "selling". Over the years, I have heard many lawyers claim that what they do is not selling but "business development". While many people may have a problem with the word selling, they are indeed selling their services. Learning to get past their phobia of the word "selling" and learning to market their skills is a key requirement for lawyers. The lawyers who do learn these skills are the ones who make it to the top. It is not necessary that a lawyer be great at law, but it is necessary that a lawyer be good at law as well as good at marketing themselves.

Your Role in All This

So what's your role in all this talk of marketing, mining and networking? For you to profit from the legal profession, you need to learn who to market to, what to market, and how to market to them. You need to learn how to effectively mine the legal gold that is present in the mine called "the legal business" and this book can teach you how to effectively do so.

I am certain that you will find success once you learn how to market to and work with lawyers. Many Coaches, Trainers and Consultants have great value yet many of you struggle to find clients and develop a viable and successful business. Lawyers have huge training budgets and will buy these services if they are marketed, priced and sold appropriately. There is no place where lawyers and HR professionals in law can find out about coaching services and access the services provided by coaches who know about the legal profession.

How to Tap into the Legal Profession

Lawyers need to thrive in the current economy, they need coaching to help them achieve this and the coaches who train them for this success, will profit, also. So once you get started you will get referrals that will ensure that you soon find the perfect client.

Diversify

Consider whether you want to diversify or expand into the legal market and whether you want to add this extra string to your bow. If you're an ex lawyer looking for a new career you might decide that you want to work exclusively with this group. Think about it - why wouldn't you want to diversify your income and add another source? We live in an increasing competitive world where technology is destroying old business models as fast as it is creating new ones. The time to diversify is now. Smart people will plan for the worst, but hope for the best.

Have a laugh

Lawyer: "Did he pick the dog up by the ears?"

Witness: "No."

Lawyer: "What was he doing with the dog's ears?"

Witness: "Picking them up in the air."

Lawyer: "Where was the dog at this time?"

Witness: "Attached to the ears."

and another...

Lawyer: "When he went, had you gone and had she, if she wanted to and were able, for the time being excluding all the restraints on her not to go, gone also, would he have brought you, meaning you and she, with him to the station?"

Other Lawyer: "Objection. That question should be taken out and shot."

Help me solve these problems

- Market myself and my firm

- Create attention towards my services

- Create products to attract clients

- Create a client base

- Manage my marketing

- Find different kinds of clients and how to manage them

- Build client relationships

- Communicate effectively with my clients

- Encourage referrals

- Stay in the know of what's new in marketing

- Carve a niche

- Build influence amongst my prospects

- Take some good photographs that reflect my image and brand

Now do something!
Knowledge is potential power.
Action is real power!

What 3 actions could you take right now?

1. _____

   _____

   _____

2. _____

   _____

   _____

3. _____

   _____

   _____

Chapter 6 - Coaching and Mentoring

I know I don't need to sell you on the benefits of coaching but this chapter breaks it down for you so that you can explain it in your marketing to give you an insight into the other areas that might not be your specialism. This chapter sets out the different types of coaching and mentoring that is available and that you can offer. My specialism within the legal market are judges, Queens Counsel and senior lawyers wanting to join their ranks. I am often asked by Chambers and law firms to recommend other coaches who can assist more junior staff or senior solicitors within big firms.

Eric Schmidt the former CEO of Google said "The best advice I ever got was to get a coach. So I have a coach. Everyone needs a coach. Every famous athlete. Every famous performer has a coach. Someone who can give you perspective. One thing people are not good at is seeing themselves as other people see them. A coach really really helps them".

Mentoring

Mentors bring expertise alongside an individual to enable them to develop insight, understanding, judgment and personal qualities such as self-confidence, and to do this faster and with fewer errors than if they were by themselves.

The core proposition of mentoring is to assist the individual in delivering effective results for their employers through accelerated leaning and/or the testing and development of their ideas by an experienced outsider. The process of mentoring is often used to describe situations where a person with sufficient experience guides, advises and transfers knowledge/thinking help to another. There are two separately recognizable processes in the coaching arena: the coaching process and the mentoring process. The first decision to be made when making a mentoring choice is that of the needed expertise, which could be one type, or many.

If political knowledge as in how to work the organizations systems to advantage is the need, then an experienced senior manager from within the organization, but out of the individuals reporting line, is the right choice.

Central to the mentoring process is understanding your own character and how it differs from those of others. In so doing, not only will you improve your own style but understand how to get the most out of your coachee.

If professional expertise, such as law, is needed then an experienced professional in or outside the organization is an appropriate choice. An outsider will bring new ideas and may also help with the politics of the organization.

Many executives want the benefit of an external, experienced leader who brings general and maybe specific business perspective, knowledge and expertise. Someone who can be used as a confidential sounding board when there is no one in the organization to play that role.

Depending on the purposes of specific mentoring, the process will differ. An internal mentor may work closely and specifically with an individual for a particular period as they step up into a new role and then fall back to be a trusted source of advice over a long period.

A mentor that brings professional expertise will probably work with an individual for a set period of time and work to specific goals.

The general business mentor will work more or less closely with a manager depending on the perceived needs of the manager. It will be a fluctuating but potentially long-running relationship.

Regardless of the nature of the relationship and process, there needs to be a clearly understood purpose, and goals that are reviewed on an agreed basis.

Ex lawyers and those who no longer wish to practice law can train to become mentors and offer this service back to the profession.

Confidentiality

Given the sensitivity of the content of the relationships you build with your lawyer clients it is important that you keep the details of your dealings with any lawyer confidential.

Have a laugh

Lawyer: "So, after the anesthesia, when you came out of it, what did you observe with respect to your scalp?"

Witness: "I didn't see my scalp the whole time I was in the hospital."

Lawyer: "It was covered?"

Witness: "Yes, bandaged."

Lawyer: "Then, later on...what did you see?"

Witness: "I had a skin graft. My whole buttocks and leg were removed and put on top of my head."

and another...

Lawyer: "Was that the same nose you broke as a child?"

Witness: "I only have one, you know."

Help me if you can

- Manage my time so I can produce more
- Set goals to make more money and have less stress
- Stop procrastinating
- Manage my needs and wants
- Motivate myself
- Build self confidence
- Set and achieve goals
- Value and enjoy my work
- Have Purpose and passion
- Prioritize my work
- Get focused

Now do something!

Knowledge is potential power.
Action is real power!

What 3 actions could you take right now?

1. _____

_____

_____

2. _____

_____

_____

3. _____

_____

_____

Chapter 7 - Types of Coaching

There are many different types of coaches and areas that you can coach lawyers in. Here are some: bereavement, business, divorce; executive, financial management, personal, sales, social media, branding, health, marketing and many other areas in which you can niche yourself. You can focus on coaching women returners, people nearing retirement. Whatever field of coaching you are in you should make your client feel like they are a super hero!

There are three main categories of coaching and there are sub-categories within each.

In this section I will look at the main three generic coaching areas and apply them to lawyers.

1. Personal Coaching (Life coaching)

As a personal coach you may niche yourself in any number of areas and use your training to help people solve a variety of problems lawyers may have. In this category I include divorce, time management, setting and achieving goals, healers, and hypnotherapists. If you help people get from where they are (usually stuck) to where they want be then I include you here.

Some personal coaches use the "Wheel of Life" and your clients can segment different areas of their lives. Segmentation is according to the percentage awarded by the client based on how happy or satisfied they are with their lives. The segment scores are then "joined up" to make a wheel.

Usually people find that their wheel is out of balance; this may explain why their lives are out of balance. The imbalances are because many people either focus too much on their personal lives; negatively impacting their professional lives, or focus too much on their professional lives, negatively impacting their personal lives.

With the wheel completed clients then choose how and where they want to be; the coach's role is to work with them to achieve this, usually on one category at a time. The process will include setting SMART goals and an action plan to achieve them. Each meeting after that session will be to check progress and for accountability; to deal with any challenges or problems that prevent the client from achieving their goals and to recognize goals that have been achieved.

You will find that lawyers work very long hours. This means that their personal lives will be negatively impacted. There is a very high divorce rate amongst lawyers. The suicide rate is also higher than average and increasing. Many lawyers drink a lot of alcohol and some develop alcohol dependency. This group may require a different type of professional assistance. Within this model of coaching there are some specifics.

The six main human emotional needs

Some coaches use the model of the six human needs to help clients have a better understanding of who they are and their main drivers. It is said that there are six main human emotional needs. You can help your client find ways to identify and fulfill these needs in a positive way. : if you can show a lawyer that you can help fulfill one of these needs, then you will have a new client. . I have found in my marketing that significance is the need that is prominent amongst most lawyers. You might choose to make these needs a focus of your marketing campaign

i.   Significance

Status and the respect of their peers are important to lawyers. The first emotional need everyone has is the need to feel significant. There is no one in the world who'll say: "It's OK for me to feel I have no value in my community and useless!" Lawyers are naturally competitive and it is very important for them to be respected and acknowledged by their peers, their company, society and friends.

During my personal coaching experience of lawyers, especially barristers and trial attorneys, they have stressed that this emotional fulfillment is incredibly important to them. So, if you feel that your coaching can help a lawyer rise in the respect of others, then highlight this in your marketing message or your sales process! Whenever I put "status" in the headline of my marketing emails the open and response rate doubles!

I put some of this desire for status or "posturing" down to the adversarial nature of our system of dispute resolution.

As a coach you can help them get to the bottom of the beliefs that are driving them and perhaps they will decide to rise above this.

Later on in their careers if they apply for judicial office or to become a Queen's Counsel then Judges and other barristers will be asked to provide assessments of their performance. They feel they cannot show any sign of weakness.

ii.   Growth

Everyone needs to feel that they are not permanently stuck in a rut, or at the same point in their lives. They need to feel that they are growing either as a person, or as a professional.

Personal growth can be described by things such as establishing your family, buying your own house, buying your first car etc.

Professional growth is defined by things such as learning more about the field that you are in, rising higher on the job ladder, being recognized for your work and so forth.

Growth helps people feel satisfied and happy with their lives, which is why everyone craves it. If your coaching will help lawyers achieve this, make sure they know.

iii. Variety

Conversely people like a degree of unpredictability. They like adventure; they like to know that there will be something to look forward to. They like surprise. No one wants to do the same thing over and over again, so if your services or product are different than the rest, and then point it out!

Prove that you're willing to go the extra mile, and that your product isn't just the same thing painted a different color, but a unique service with unique characteristics. Find out what their passions are. So they can get variety in other areas of their lives if they are not getting much at work.

iv. Certainty

People want to feel that they are in control of their lives. They want to feel that they are the master of their lives and that no one can take that from them. Being in control of their lives could mean anything from paying bills on time, to knowing they will be able to send their children to private schools to making sure they bring in enough work to keep the employed associates busy.

While everyone has different ways of controlling their lives, ensure you're your product supports their aspirations and that you can deliver more control to their lives. This human need is primary for many people in corporate firms.

v. Contribution

Lawyers like to contribute to others. They take part in various types of charity work in order to learn more about the community that they live in and as a way to give back to their community. It also helps them build a positive reputation in the society that they live in as this can help their businesses grow and profit. There is a Bar Pro Bono Unit that provides free legal assistance to those who cannot afford it. Law firms also undertake pro bono activities.

If you are involved in pro bono activities or if you can help them manage their time so that they have more time to be involved in their community then tell them!

vi. Love and Connection

All human beings desire to be loved. They desire to be appreciated, and to feel a human connection with others. In business, it is important for a lawyer to not only connect with the people that he or she works for but also with the people that they work with.

You can help teams connect to deliver on the project. If positive connection is missing people will get it through other means which may not be as positive for them.

2. Executive Coaching

As the phrase "executive coach" is used so widely in the business world, its definition varies from place to place. The following is a widely accepted definition. Coaching is the art of facilitating the performance, learning and development of another person, within an organizational context.

Executive coaching involves the use of non-directive coaching and mentoring. A great coach can do both coaching and mentoring where appropriate - but it is quite rare for a mentor to have the specific skills to coach in a non-directive way.

The Processes

The core proposition of coaching is to assist the individual in delivering effective results for their employers - through learning, attitudinal and behavioral change, environmental change etc.

Coaching remains as much an art as a science - best practiced by individuals with acute perception diplomacy, sound judgment and the ability to navigate conflicts with integrity. And, most importantly, non-directed; the coach's role is to facilitate the individual to drive the learning process themselves.

What is the coaching process?

The client must firstly ask and answer the key question: what is the point of an investment in coaching? In other words, how will coaching further the attainment of key business goals? Why? Because coaching is not always the right tool to use.

Executive coaching success rates are likely to rise if the 3 parties in the process - the client (employer), the individual (employee) and the coach - agree the SMART (Specific, Measurable, Achievable, Realistic and Timed) goals for the coaching outcomes up-front.

Most importantly, the individual must want to be coached - and be confident that his/her efforts to become more self-aware and change behaviors will be appreciated and encouraged by their line manager and key colleagues. Real commitment from the individual to targeted change is paramount.

Openness and directness in this 3 way discussion has enormous value - clear boundaries around the roles of the parties and confidentiality can be established in a business like, matter of fact way. These are the key elements of an effective coaching contract.

The coaching process needs to be properly managed and coherent to all involved. Coherence means a simple but robust process of planning what success would look like and setting goals doing and practicing, and achieving and measuring specific deliverables that are sustained and built on.

Having too many goals should be avoided - three is often a good target and these should be included in the coaching agreement that all three parties sign up to. It is necessary that these goals be driven by business imperatives and with demonstrable commitment from the top.

Customized 360 degree feedback processes, aligned to the specific coaching goals can be valuable in evaluating the perception of key people to changes in approach, behavior of the coached.

Business Coaching for the Sole Practitioner

Business coaching involves coaching an individual or a team with responsibility for the growth of a business owner, entrepreneur or solopreneur. The old image that people used to have of coaching with "scented candles and hand-holding" has been replaced with a new found respect. Some coaches are invited to sit in on board meetings and strategy summits.

Business coaches can help the business owner to feel less lonely. Running a law practice is a solitary role. It also comes with a great deal of responsibility over and above that felt by other business owners. Of course, they talk to their team, but they can't share everything with them, nor would they share their innermost concerns.

Have A Laugh

Lawyer: "Now, you have investigated other murders, have you not, where there was a victim?"

and another...

Lawyer: "Now, doctor, isn't it true that when a person dies in his sleep, in most cases he just passes quietly away and doesn't know anything about it until the next morning?"

and another...

Lawyer: "And what did he do then?"

Witness: "He came home, and next morning he was dead."

Lawyer: "So when he woke up the next morning he was dead?"

Help me with these

- Be successful in an interview
- Impress my managers and get recognized
- Create a positive image at work
- Become a Partner in my firm
- Become a Judge
- Become a Queens Counsel
- Survive the "Sausage Machine".

Now do something!

Knowledge is potential power.
Action is real power!

What 3 actions could you take right now?

1. _____

_____

_____

2. _____

_____

_____

3. _____

_____

_____

Chapter 8 - Benefits of a Coach

Some coaches don't value themselves enough. If you are one of these then this chapter will refresh you and hopefully rekindle your passion for your craft.

Coaching Spend

In the US alone it is estimated that companies spend $1 billion annually on coaching. Forbes has stated that "As more and more people begin to question the value of debt-fueled, formalized, frequently-out-of-touch academic education, will personalized one-on-one coaching—often over phone or Skype video chat, and often far cheaper and more targeted than many college courses—become a new form of education for the 21st century?" Forbes.com

The legal training market is worth billions. You are in a very good place as a coach. The coaching profession will continue to grow. Make sure you grow your practice with it.

Coaching and the bottom line

Studies are emerging that quantify the bottom line benefit of coaching. The Chartered Institute of Personal Development (CIPD) survey on coaching and buying coaching services also found that ninety nine percent of respondents believed coaching can deliver tangible benefits to individuals and organizations.

Ninety six percent of respondents believed coaching is an effective way of promoting learning in organizations. Ninety two percent of respondents believed that when coaching is managed effectively it can have a positive impact on the bottom line.

Manchester Consulting Inc estimated an average return on

investment of $100k on each coaching assignment (at a return of 5.7 times expenditure). Metrix Global calculated a 529% return on investment alongside significant intangible benefits. Both of these studies are referenced in the CIPD report.

Some figures show that with training alone (even if done very effectively) there may be an improvement of just over 20% in performance and productivity. If the training is re-enforced with coaching the improvements increase sharply to well over 80%.

The Xerox Corporation found that if they did not deliver follow-up coaching, people lost 87% of the skills change brought about from training. Many firms can benefit from more candor and less denial.

Lawyers want to increase the bottom line. You can help them. Use these studies in your marketing, along with your testimonials, to demonstrate to them the benefit. You can help them to become and remain clear and focused on their goals and targets.

Here are some things that lawyers may want and need from a coach:

To make their firms more like a business

- Business to work the way they want

- Efficient staff

- Happy spouse and family

- Good health

- Consistent income

- Succession plan - a plan for them to exit the business

Top lawyers are increasingly troubled by this conundrum: how to balance their business effectively and their own well-being / home life. Increasingly, they are prepared to look for answers and coaching is one of the things they are looking at. A business coach can become an important part of the team.. You too can become your clients' "secret weapon" and help them see and change their role as a leader and business person for the better.

Lawyers and senior executives say that spending a few sessions with a coach has a real impact. Comments include how a good executive coach can help them: to work 50% more on their business and 50% less in their business; help them to increase their profits; have 50% more time for themselves and their family AND make them 100% happier.

In the past few years' executive coaching has ballooned: the International Coach Federation, the industry's trade body, now has 7,500 members in 35 countries, including 650 in the UK. Their services are not cheap - coaching may cost £20,000 for a down payment, £10,000 per quarter and as much as £3,000 a day for individual attention. But the results have impressed British boards so much that they are not just paying the bills but increasingly insisting that all executives enroll. Companies that have embraced the coaching culture include Unilever, BP, National Grid, Northern Foods, Reuters and KPMG. Law firms include Freshfields, Allen & Overy, Herbert Smith and Norton Rose.

More and more business decisions are being made with the help of a silent coach in the background.

Having a coach is sometimes seen as a sign of weakness. But among lawyers it is becoming more acceptable. If the lawyer is confident enough to recognize when they need to talk, it makes them a good leader. One small firm I worked with was going through a tough time, losing money and being intensely scrutinized. The owner valued the experience and wise sounding-board that I was able to provide. It has been demonstrated that a coach can have a stunning impact on a business.

Be aware though that while many executives embrace coaching, others are becoming alarmed at the strong but invisible -

and unaccountable - influence coaches might have. You will probably be asked to sign a strict confidentiality agreement to protect the law firms' clients and data.

When John Dunsmore took over as chief executive of Scottish Courage, the British arm of Scottish & Newcastle, in 2002, he considered himself an easy-going chap. He knew he had a difficult task ahead - it was his first top position at a FTSE 100 company and the company's shares were plunging ever deeper in the bear market. (The Economist)

So when human resources suggested he have a natter with a business mentor, he agreed. "I've always welcomed straightforward feedback on my management style," he said. "I didn't know what to expect, but I was interested." This is how influential you as a coach can become to a business.

As a coach you can help the coachee to focus on her/his work and style. Although you spend most of your time listening and asking questions there are times when you can present your client with some arresting home truths. If you have built a relationship of trust, they will accept your feedback.

The higher you get in corporate life, the less you are questioned, particularly on a personal scale. It's not easy to just start talking openly about your work and life. Trust has to be earned and developed. Similarly with a small firm or business owner it is hard to ask for and accept help so when they do ask for your help you will need to develop and demonstrate that you can be trusted.

As a coach you can see things the business owner cannot. You are standing from the sideline so you can see the whole game. You can feedback on how they are leading the team, are they delegating enough and appropriately. How do they appoint a team and support it to operate effectively. What is the belief behind their hiring strategy and technique? For example are they hiring people like them who they got on with, rather than those who were needed because they had different skills? You can be the invaluable third-party impartial sounding- board helping them to survive in choppy waters.

Profiling Tools

As an Executive or Business coach you can make use of various profiling tools to help your client get a better understanding of how they make decisions. There are several including Myers-Briggs, one of the better known, is a grid with 16 characteristic profiles to help you understand your method of being and working. Other popular systems are Centaur and DISC.

Centaur is an adapted psychological system which can be used for developing corporate leadership. The idea is that people in a business environment fit into five broad personality types, each with preferred ways of relating to the world. Managers should treat each type differently in order to assist their growth and hence their performance and productivity. The basic problem with us all is we treat people like ourselves. But if managers want the best results, they must understand how to bring the best out of employees.

The Centaur system is rooted in the belief that we develop the fundamental part of our personality before we are five years old. By this age we have become entrenched in how we see ourselves and others. If we can understand this, we can understand our behavior, character and reactions.

For example, using the chart, if you are a "warrior", you generally speak your mind. But if a "warrior" boss approached a "wizard" employee in this way, it would frighten him and sap his confidence. Equally, if a "wizard" took his gentle approach to a "superhero" the latter would be impatient or take offence at what he perceived as patronizing behavior.

It may seem woolly but executives are finding that this system works. Richard Bentley, joint head of the International Coach Federation, said: "An effective executive seeks to identify the potential of his or her team and how to grow that potential to the advantage of the individual and the organization."

Independent articles in the Law Society Gazette attests to the growing confidence that lawyers, partners, and HR professionals in law place upon coaching as a developmental tool. Further, an article in the Times Newspaper also catalogues the awesome results that coaches are helping business owners and executives to achieve. A partner at Herbert Smith, one of the top law firms in the City of London, said "I can't think of a time when I will not use a coach".

How to work with lawyers - my personal experiences

Have a heart of gold.

I've heard people use the phrase "she has a heart of gold" but I never really thought about what it meant until now. One of the lines in Neil Young's song says: "I've been a miner for a heart of gold". Gold is hard. So how can one have a heart of gold? Well, what I have learned is that pure gold is actually a relative soft metal. It is usually mixed with other metals to make it hard and more durable. So, to me, having a heart of gold means that if people are going to trust you with their innermost fears, frustrations, thoughts, and weaknesses then you must be sincere, generous, genuine, authentic and respectful. This has been my key to success in this market.

This book is not for gold diggers. It is not for people who take and don't give. But it is for gold seekers. Those who want to succeed and support others in their success; those who come from a space of giving and loving.

People can spot a phony. Lawyers have been described as sharks. However, in all my experience of coaching and consulting and training I have never coached a shark. When I was in the City, however I did see lawyers who I would describe as having "shark like" tendencies but the majority are sincere. Some are just playing out their beliefs and their lack of security. But whilst they got results they never struck me as being happy. Some of them often had "complicated" personal relationships.

Most coaches, trainers and consultants I have met have a heart of gold. When someone gives you the honor of allowing you to assist them. When someone says to you. "Help me solve this problem", it is the most heartwarming feeling. When they ask you to hold their hand as they go through a trauma, or challenge, it is humbling. When they ask me to be their comfort blanket for a few months. My heart melts.

When a barrister or solicitor who earns over $1million a year asks you to do this and trusts you with their time, energy and passion and commitment for several months to help them achieve even more success, I cannot describe the feeling. Alright then, as I am writing this book I will describe the feeling. At first you may feel fear. You may think to yourself "I only earn a quarter of what you earn". "I'm younger than you". "What can I possibly add to you that you don't already have".

But then they let you into their world and give you a glimpse of their challenges. As I write this part of the book there are tears in my eyes. Tears, because my challenges in life are able to help someone else overcome theirs. Tears, because someone trusted me to help them achieve success. I'm sure you have had that same feeling. You connect with the heart and soul of your client. As you support them or lead them to where they want to go to achieve their life's goals. It is truly an honor.

Most of you as coaches or consultants will have experienced this feeling. If you are in HR and work with lawyers I hope you too experience this and never lose that ability to truly connect with people.

Who Coaches the Coach?

If you don't already have a coach or a mentor, or mastermind group, I strongly suggest you get one or several to coach you through different areas of your life and business. You need to download. As you support others, you need to be receiving support. Your clients pay you to also take care of yourself, so make sure that you invest some of the money back into you.

Someone once told me the difference between helping and supporting. If you "help" someone you are somehow attached to their success or failure, and you are emotionally affected. On the other hand if you "support" them then you still give them your best but you are not personally attached to the outcome of whether they succeed or not.

It's been said that "like attracts like". So if you have a heart of gold then you will attract like minded people.

Have a laugh

Lawyer: "So the date of conception (of the baby) was August 8th?"

Witness: "Yes!"

Lawyer: "And what were you doing at that time?"

Help me if you can

- Build a cost efficient office

- Cultivate efficiency

- Create employment policies

- Create and maintain records and databases

- Manage my business and my team efficiently

- Develop business strategies

Now do something!
Knowledge is potential power.
Action is real power!

What 3 actions could you take right now?

1. _____

   _____

   _____

2. _____

   _____

   _____

3. _____

   _____

   _____

SECTION III -
Go Prospecting

When the gold rush happened, California had been a very sparsely populated area. However, once the news spread that gold had been found, one of the largest migrations in human history took place. People walked, rode and sailed to California in order to gain a part of the fortune.

The people who came out the richest were the two workers building a sawmill near Sacramento. These two workers had discovered the presence of gold, and they were the ones who had made it big.

The point of this is that in order to make it big, you have to start out doing the hard work. You can't just sit in your chair and expect clients to walk in through the door. You have to market your services exactly right so that clients are attracted to your business.

Chapter 9 - Prepare Your Tools

Lawyers are very conscious of people attempting to sell them all kinds of stuff. At the same time I have found that they are generally very polite and open to listening. Barristers, in particular, are quite open-minded. However, you can market your services in a way that guarantees that the doors will be opened to you. So how can you market your service to them? The exact same way that you would market your services to any other clients! Albeit, with some minor twists.

So what tools will you need to market to lawyers?

Set a Clear Intention

Be clear what you want your marketing to bring you. So set a goal, whether it's lead generation, product selling, or brand management. It is much easier to work on your marketing once you have a clear goal in mind.

Understand Expectations

All customers have certain expectations when purchasing services from someone. In the same way, your lawyer prospects have certain expectations which you must understand to prevent costly assumptions, and create a profitable, referring, and enjoyable client base. It is claimed that business is all about expectation, and the legal business is no exception. Tell them what results they will get by working with you. Most lawyers want a combination or all of the following: more money, more time, less stress and a balanced life.

Have a Clear Sales Process

While often times, it is not easy to analyze your own work, it is necessary that you learn to do this. In fact, since we are our own toughest critic, if you feel that you are satisfied by what you have set out in your sales plan, your clients are more than likely to be satisfied with it as well. Review your sales plan with the following guidelines in mind.

What expectations do you set? Do you meet all these expectations? Which do you fail to meet? Which do you deliver against, and how often do you attempt to exceed expectations? What impact does this have on the people around you?

Set SMART Goals

While goals are necessary to accomplishing anything, this does not mean that if you set a goal you will accomplish it. The best way to achieve meeting your goals is to set SMART goals where your goals are Specific, Measurable, Achievable, Realistic and Time based. Creating a SMART goal increases your chance of realizing said goal, as well as your chances of even exceeding expectations and delivering above and beyond the goal that you set for yourself.

Deliver your Service to a Consistently High Standard

The main focus of a business is not only to attract new clients, but to keep the ones that you attract. To do this, you must not only set clear expectations from the start but you must continue to meet these expectations over and over again.

It is often said that 80% of your profit comes from 20% of the clients, and these are the clients who are thoroughly satisfied with your service. To keep these clients around, it is necessary that you consistently keep your service at a high level.

Have a laugh

Lawyer: "Any suggestions as to what prevented this from being a murder trial instead of an attempted murder trial?"

Witness: "The victim lived."

and another...

Lawyer: "Doctor, before you performed the autopsy, did you check for a pulse?"

Witness: " No."

Lawyer: "Did you check for blood pressure?"

Witness: "No."

Lawyer: "Did you check for breathing?"

Witness: " No."

Lawyer: "So, then it is possible that the patient was alive when you began the autopsy?"

Witness: "No."

Lawyer: "How can you be so sure, Doctor?"

Witness: " Because his brain was sitting on my desk in a jar."

Lawyer: "But could the patient have still been alive, nevertheless?"

Witness: "Yes, it is possible that he could have been alive and practicing law somewhere

Help me If You Can

Career Progression

- Perfect my pitch
- Write and publish my book

Business Planning

- Plan my new business for success
- Review my existing business
- Balance my home and work life
- Prepare for maternity leave, stay connected and return to work after my baby
- Live up to my full potential

Now do something!
Knowledge is potential power.
Action is real power!

What 3 actions could you take right now?

1. _____

_____

_____

2. _____

_____

_____

3. _____

_____

_____

Chapter 10 - Set out Your Stall with Elegant Marketing

The process of marketing whether by word of mouth, internet, social media, TV, sales flyers, or billboards, has one goal: to build a community of consumers. A community is a group of like minded people with common interests, goals, and values, who, as a result, are more prone to buying certain products and services.

The real purpose of marketing is to identify and build a community of consumers who seek the services that you provide. These consumers also need to have to resources to pay for your services so that your business does not go into loss. You will find success once you learn how to market to and work with lawyers. Many Coaches, Trainers and Consultants have great value to offer yet many of them struggle to find clients and develop a viable and successful business. Lawyers have huge training budgets and will buy these services if they are marketed, priced and sold appropriately. There is no place where lawyers and HR professionals in law can find out about coaching services and access the services provided by coaches who know about the legal profession, so you have to bring your services to their attention.

Training budgets

The legal training budget in the UK alone is worth several billion. There are three major players in the legal training market, but the rest are relatively small companies usually comprising of one main coach or trainer who brings in associates to help them deliver on a project.

Remember, marketing isn't about doing the same thing as everyone/anyone or even someone else, and hoping that your customer sees that you are a better option. To market yourself successfully, you have to stand out from the crowd, you have to shout above the noise by making a unique impression that gets a response.

I read the following in LinkedIn and had to laugh. "I remember when I was at school I always wondered how come some of the ugliest boys, the ones with the biggest noses and the thickest eyebrows in town were doing so well with the girls. Being a relatively pretty boy I simply could not understand why the girls chose them over me. I now know that there is something about a very big nose which makes it stand out from the rest of the crowd. Once the girls come to check your big nose out, personality takes over." It explained so graphically how you need to market yourself in today's world to get noticed. It may seem silly, but this is very true: Seth Godin refers to this as the "Purple Cow" in his book. So show your personality and stand out! Then be outstanding!

Now that you know how to market to lawyers, you must learn what media you can use to market to lawyers. It is important to keep your marketing medium relevant to your target demographic; in the same way that you wouldn't market to teenagers using newspapers, know which resources reach lawyers effectively. The three main distribution sources most attractive to lawyers are:

Direct Mail

This is still a very effect method of reaching lawyers, attorneys and HR professionals in law firms. When you write to a lawyer or attorney directly, hand write the envelope and put a stamp on it. Write at the top of the envelope capitalized in blue ink. "PRIVATE AND CONFIDENTIAL FOR THE ATTENTON OF ADDRESSEE ONLY". This will almost guarantee that it will not be opened by anyone, except the addressee. If you are approaching a firm then write to three or four people in the firm. The Senior Partner and the Partner responsible for training/ marketing/ trainees, whatever your particular focus is. Send the next two letters to the Head of HR and the Learning and Development Manager or the Training Manager. Call the firm and find out who has these roles, if it is not clear from the website. In fact, call anyway just in case the website is out of date. Address the letter to the person by name. And again use the "Private and Confidential" words above. Make sure it is handwritten in blue ink.

The bulk of each letter will be the same. But change the letter to appeal to the particular drivers, needs and concerns of the individual according to their position in the company. Generally, Partners are concerned about increasing revenue and reducing costs (remember the extra money goes straight to their pockets). HR will be interested in reducing churning, or whatever the current worry is. HR will usually control the budget for training. They will have a strategy, so find out how your offer fits the strategy. The Learning and Development manager will be familiar with the development needs of individuals in the firm and will be closer to the coal face.

If you do this, then you increase the chances of your letter getting to the person it is addressed to unopened. This in itself will be of interest to them as most of their other post will have been opened by the people in the post room or their secretaries. It is likely that the Senior Partner will read your letter and pass it on to HR or Learning and Development with a comment. Follow up with all four people. Ask if they received your letter. Begin the sales process.

Email marketing and Internet presence

Of course ensure that you have a comprehensive and helpful website and social media presence. They will check you out before they call you.

Sales flyers are very often thrown away, or discarded without even a glance at what was being sold. They can also be regarded as a waste of resources, since the audience didn't even look at the advert. You can take out an advert in a newspaper or a magazine. Lawyers have their personal or political preference of newspapers, but most read the Times and the Financial Times. There are not many magazines and journals that focus on the legal business. The main ones in the UK are: The Lawyer, Legal Week, The Law Journal, The Law Gazette, New Law Journal, and Counsel Magazine (read religiously by barristers). Write an article or get featured in one of these.

Cold Calling

Cold calling has for a long time, been one of the most prevalent methods of marketing. However, if done incorrectly, cold calls can give your business a bad reputation and discourage lawyers from seeking you to provide services. So there are a few tips which need to be followed when cold calling lawyers. However, keep in mind that these are general guidelines and if you are looking for more in detail descriptions you can refer to the various books on sales and selling.

The first and most important tip: you must do it elegantly! Do not be too pushy when you call a lawyer. Remember, the purpose of marketing is for the lawyer to remember your services and purchase them because they are suited to them, not purchase them because they were being forced by a harassing cold caller. But if, like me, you believe with certainty that they can benefit from your services then it is your duty to bring their attention to that fact. Then it is their choice.

Be the Secretary's Friend

Be polite to the receptionist or secretary. It is near impossible that a lawyer will attend to all the calls they receive by themselves so you need to get past the receptionist in order to talk to the actual lawyer. The best way to do this is to be polite, and impressive, and your call will soon be put through to the lawyer.

Always keep in mind that lawyers are very busy people and that it's best to call them really early in the day - most lawyers start working at 7am - if you want to catch them free for a direct conversation.

Even if you are unable to connect to the lawyer, do not just hang up! Leave a message. While you may think that there is no chance that a lawyer would call back a cold caller, it is entirely possible. The key to getting a call back is to leave a message that indicates that they will gain from a call back, for example, saying that you have some important news.

Remain polite and charming. It is necessary that even if you don't make a deal right away, you make a good impression, increasing the chances of a lawyer considering your company if they do decide to purchase the services that you offer.

Internet Marketing

The internet is an ever growing phenomenon and as such, it gives you the best way to promote services to your clients. It allows you to give your message to a large number of people without any cost at all! One drawback is that most lawyers are very cautious about opening up to social media and the internet.

Robert Cialdini wrote the book "Influence: The Psychology of Persuasion" in 2007 and it's remained a business best seller ever since. The six principles of influence he writes about apply even more so to working with lawyers as they do not have a great deal of time to search the internet.

These principles need to form the cornerstone of your sales, marketing and particularly online persuasion, where you have minimal time to capture the lawyers' attention and persuade them to take up your offerings.

The Six Rules of Persuasion are:

1. Authority

2. Likeability

3. Commitment & Consistency

4. Reciprocity

5. Social Proof

6. Scarcity

All of these elements are needed to make up a on and off line marketing campaign and to generate interest in your business.

These days one of the best ways to spread your message on the internet is via social media. However, the bad news is there do not seem to be many lawyers on social media sites. There are a variety of reasons for this. Lawyers are very risk averse. A number of firms ban their staff from using social media sites whilst at work as people spend too much time on them and also the risk of them posting inappropriate messages whilst at work. Many lawyers do use LinkedIn, however.

Social media and networking platforms like Facebook, Twitter and LinkedIn are receiving lots of attention as tools for Business

Development and Client Attraction - and it's easy to spend a lot of (wasted) time there. To attract ideal high paying lawyers from social media, it's important to remember that that the same rules apply for social media as they do for traditional marketing: give value and build relationships!

One personal experience of internet abuse happened in 1998 when I was in private practice. Some of my male colleagues were downloading pornography; they were all gathered around the computer and laughing. As I walked past their desk I glimpsed some well known cartoon characters doing some unspeakable things. Now this would be an offence and most likely result in the sack. I still remember this13 years later. So perhaps lawyers are right to want to rein in their employees while they are at work.

The modern increase in social media has brought a whole new trouble with it. Workers waste valuable time online "tweeting", "liking" or other such activities instead of their work. Even more challenging, they may post offensive tweets that can compromise another person or the firm's reputation and be labeled as libel or slander. If the offence is committed during working time then the firm could be liable.

To protect themselves from this kind of behavior, law firms have developed long policies on social network. I have a friend who currently works in a medium sized law firm who tells me there is a 30 page policy for staff on how to use social media.

How to get the most out of Social Media

Here are some tips that are specific to attracting lawyers and others. Remember your aim is to attract prospects, build the relationship and hopefully turn them into life time clients.

Create great relevant content that adds value to your audience that it motivates them to take further action into working with you.

When using social media, you want to be clear on how you can tap into this new marketing strategy and still remain "Client Attractive." Here are some strategies for doing so:

1. Have a clear objective and develop a strategy.

   Due to the popularity of sites like Facebook and Twitter - it's easy to get sucked into the "bright shiny object syndrome" and immediately jump in 100% by using these tools as a way to market your business and attract clients.

   You need to have an objective. Is it to build your list? Attract more clients? Position yourself in the marketplace with more prospects and potential joint venture partners? What call-to-action or response do you want to achieve with each interaction with social media? Get clear on your end result first - then develop the plan.

2. Focus on long-term relationship development.

   Marketing is not about a quick approach to building relationships - and it's no different in social media platforms. It takes time to cultivate relationships with prospects before they become clients. Prospects through social media still want to know you and like you and ultimately trust you before they decide to work with you or buy your product.

   Through the power of social media you can deepen that connection and build the bond with the person you're relating with. You can accelerate that relationship or expand your reach with the amazing "connectivity" that social media provides - but you must remain focused on that relationship and connection you build over time in order to remain client attractive.

3. It's not about you, it's about them.

   Because literally anyone can tap into connections through social media - you need to be extra client attractive and stand out from the crowd. To "cut through the clutter" and ensure your message and your connection remains on the top of the radar with your potential clients, it's important to focus on giving before you expect to get anything in return.

Deliver the same 'high-value' and 'high-content' information that you do in your articles, emails and on your website. Social media is no different; when you show your connections you add even MORE value, and your prospects will be attracted to you.

4. Be genuine, real and transparent.

In case you haven't noticed a theme here, it's this: Social media is all about connection. People want to connect with you in so many ways like they would in real-life. Be who you are on Facebook and Twitter as you would be face-to-face. Even though it's online, people can still see through the "fake" of social media just like they could if they meet someone in person. The more you "show up" as the real you in social media - the more people will want to connect with you and be interested in building that relationship even further.

Have integrity with everything you do with social media. Remember this: Never post anything through social media that you wouldn't want blasted on a motorway billboard or the front page of the *Daily Mail* for the entire world to see.

5. Social media is all about the conversation - happening online.

If you're not showing up and contributing to the conversation that is taking place - you'll never leverage the true power of social media and build a client attractive business. It's not a one-sided conversation where you just continually promote yourself and not engage with anyone in your network.

Social media and networking is no different from in-person networking. It's a two-way conversation for you AND the other person - that's what creates the value. When you contribute and collaborate with your audience, they will respect you and be more attracted to you.

6. Be consistent and plan your time.

    Social media could suck you in and drain all your time very easily and quickly. Before you know it - you've spent half the day on Facebook and Twitter and you've not added one person to your list or engaged any new potential prospects, let alone got any "real" work done.

    Develop a daily and weekly plan where you identify how much time you will spend on the platforms and what result you want to achieve. It's like any other slice in the Client Attraction Marketing Pie - you can't just put in half the effort and expect the full result.

    Show up consistently and contribute consistently to realize the long-term benefit.

Remember, you don't get clients from social media. You get clients through socializing on social media platforms. It's from the connections you establish, the long-term added value proposition that you provide those individuals and the way you cultivate the relationship, that they see you as an attractive expert. Focus on that and you'll never be without clients ever again.

The first step in using social media as part of your marketing strategy is to identify your overall goal and then work backwards with a detailed plan that delivers it. What is your required end result? For example, if it's to build your prospect list - then you want to develop a step-by-step strategy that allows you to engage your network with the intent of attracting people back to your website where they can get your irresistible free offer and join your list for long term relationship development.

The next step is to identify the tools and platforms that work best for you. Twitter might be extremely popular out there, but does your market actually exist in big numbers on Twitter? Lawyers, for instance are gather more in LinkedIn. Spend some time on these various platforms and determine which works best for you and your niche.

The final step is to turn up and do the work to a high professional standard. Social media as a marketing strategy should take some personal time and effort. You can't just set up a profile and update your status and then ask, "Why don't the clients show up?" You need to step up your activity, engage and contribute to the conversation with consistently valuable content to attract your ideal client's attention that you want to reach through social media.

Have a laugh

Lawyer: How was your first marriage terminated?

Witness: By death.

Lawyer: And by whose death was it terminated?

MAKING THE MOST OF LINKEDIN

About LinkedIn

As at September 2011 there are 100 million people on LinkedIn. They are from all over the world, so your business can be truly international. The users tend to be more business people and professionals, including attorneys and lawyers. Lawyers and HR people will look you up on LinkedIn to find out about you as a person. They may also look for you on Facebook and at your company website. Using LinkedIn is acceptable. Whether you like it or not your prospects will check you out! What will they find?

How to get the most out of LinkedIn

To get the most out of LinkedIn it is important that your page looks professional. This mean that you must use the language that your prospective clients use. They should be able to find out how you can help them to solve their problems.

LinkedIn has features and tools you can used to proactively market yourself. You don't have to sit around hoping that someone finds you. You can search for potential buyers of your services. You can get involved and connect with lawyers and HR people in the firms you want to approach.

It is a powerful tool to connect to professional prospective clients and firms. Make sure your page speaks their language. If you are not on LinkedIn then you should set up your profile as soon as you can. Make sure that your profile is complete. You can search for lawyers, law firms, barristers, attorneys. It is important though that you don't just copy your resume.

Your prospective clients will not be interested in your past jobs. They are not interested in how many people you used to manage or the size of the budget you were responsible for. All they want to know is whether you can help them solve a pressing problem that they have so tailor your profile so that it is of interest to them.

Try and get people to recommend you. It is not always easy to get people to recommend you even if they are happy with the results you have created. You may have difficulty because of the confidential nature of the work and because lawyers are very concerned about their status. Not all of them want to admit that they have asked for and received help from you. But if they give you a testimonial, you can paste it into your profile and withhold their name.

Treat LinkedIn as your individual page. Only talk about yourself and not your company. Its main purpose is to start the process of building connection with you the person. Write your profile in the first person, use "I" not "we".

It is not like a Facebook page. Do not just send people to your website. This will not make them want to connect with you. Use it to reach out to new people not just to stay in touch with friends and old colleagues. LinkedIn lets you see who your contacts' contacts are. You can search everyone you know for names, companies, firms, job titles - and it will tell you who knows them.

Invest the time in LinkedIn to develop relationships. It is better in some ways than "face to face" networking as it exposes you to more people. It can give you a direct line to your most valuable client. On LinkedIn you really do have the right people in the right place and it's not too difficult to connect with them.

But don't spend too much of your time there as it can become counter productive. Schedule the amount of time you will spend on all social media activities. Usually half an hour a day is sufficient. Have clear objectives, a strategy and a plan to implement it. I have a 30 page Internet Marketing and Social Media Strategy and Implementation plan. I read it regularly to remind me of my focus. In fact I paid a social media consultant to work with me on the development of the plan. I then add to the plan as I learn something new or discover another helpful tool.

Set up a group and join other groups. Ask questions in the groups and post answers. This will establish your expertise. Monitor the time you spend on there as it is easy to get hooked. Decide how much time you will just have fun using it and enjoy it! Don't use real business time just to chat or debate. Ask yourself whether it is bringing you the clients you need.

LinkedIn also has some Advanced Features that can be helpful.

Have a referral strategy.

Use LinkedIn to be found by others, to keep in touch and to build your credibility. This will bring you the best return. You can ask your contacts to introduce you to people you want to meet.

How do I get the most impact?

Make your profile client focused. Use your profile to let your prospect know that you understand their perspective and their concerns. Ask yourself: what does a potential client need to know about me? What problems do I solve? How am I different? Is my proposition clear? How can I demonstrate my credibility? How can I let them know that they can trust me? Use the pitch that you developed. Use a case study or a short quote from testimonial. Give your back story of your achievements, not to show off but to demonstrate your credibility. Build a story to soften it from boastfulness.

LinkedIn will tell you how many times your profile comes up in someone's search. Find out what law firms are searching for. What search words are they using and edit your profile to match what they are searching for?

As at today LinkedIn's algorithms are better than Google. If you are connected to someone on LinkedIn then you will come up higher on their search.

Your Profile

Make sure your headline is representative of what problem you solve. Have a good clear professional photograph. The default position is that LinkedIn takes your headline from your most recent job title. This is not what you want. You can go into LinkedIn and edit the headline so that it matchs your desired key word. For example "Networking Coach Providing Advice For Lawyers".

Put your key search words in the "Summary" part of the profile and under the "Previous Jobs" section. But don't proliferate your profile with key words, it is too intrusive and may put off the big firms. Remember, they are more cautious and risk averse than entrepreneurs. As you will be selling a very high value service your profile should have a high impact and give this message clearly.

Connect to Large Numbers of People

Make sure that you get connected to a large number of people who might be connected to potential buyers. Be selective. You probably won't want to be a LION (LinkedIn Open Networker). These people will connect with anyone and their objective is to connect with as many people as possible so they are not discriminating. Also be careful not to connect with too many LIONs because this gives them access to your contacts.

The alternative to a LION is a "Trusted Partner" Strategy. This is where you are more selected about who you connect to. You would only connect to people who you know and to people they know. The downside to this is that you limit the opportunities for introductions.

The other option is to go for somewhere in between the two. If someone interesting asks to connect with you then connect with them. Be alert for LIONS though and people who look like they will spam you. If there is no logical reason then question why they want to connect.

Once you are connected start the relationship. Look at their profile. Start the relationship by sending them a message saying you are happy to connect and refer to something in their profile.

Once you have established a common ground to chat and you have built the relationship you can ask for a recommendation.

You can use the Toolbar for outlook on your PC so that LinkedIn can scan your Outlook and offer to send invitations to your contacts asking them to connect with you on LinkedIn.

You should be careful how you use this tool. Only send an invitation to people you know and who you believe won't mind connecting with you. Write a tailored message using the Outlook tool bar. Have a LinkedIn signature.

Join Groups - Post and Answer Questions

Post questions and answers in the groups and ask for a connection after speaking to them in a group.

It is advisable to have around 500 connections - half of whom you know well and the other half from reaching out and connecting. This will give you a lot more visibility because you will be connected to many more people.

How to Ask For a Connection

1. Find people who you want to connect to

2. Look at people you know well and their connections - you cannot know who they are connected to.

Use the search feature and the advanced search feature to search for industry sectors. Search for people who used to work for the firms you want to connect with. You can narrow the search to people in your location.

Focus your efforts on the people who your people are connected to. It will tell you how you are connected to them. You can see the shared connection and photographs.

Start to build the relationship with these people to leverage and increase you connections. When you connect with someone do not ask for an introduction straight away. This is impersonal. Let people get to know, like and trust you. Eventually they may ask you and you can then tell them. LinkedIn is a professional network so people know that if you are on there you are interested in business contacts.

It is probably best to get on the phone have a conversation and then, if appropriate, ask for an introduction. Remember to have a clear objective in asking for the introduction. Be clear that you can add value or solve a problem for the person to whom you want to be connected. You may not know them that well so you may have to re-establish the relationship.

When you telephone them say: "Hi, I was looking at LinkedIn and I noticed that you are connected to Jane MacDonald. If you were me how would you go about getting introduced to Jane?

Get them to think like you and if they really want to give you an introduction then they will. Ask them "Would it be possible for you to introduce me to her? If they say, "Yes". Then ask them: "Would you like me to give you a few words?" If you know them really well and if they like you ask them: "Why don't we all go out for lunch?" Or just go ahead and ask for a strong referral!

Have a laugh

Lawyer: "Can you tell us what was
          stolen from your house?"

Witness: "There was a rifle that belonged
          to my father that was stolen
          from the hall closet."

Lawyer: "Can you identify the rifle?"

Witness: "Yes. There was something
          written on the side of it."

Lawyer: "And what did the writing say?"

Witness: "'Winchester'!"

Help me if you can

- Build a community of consumers who are interested in purchasing my service
- Create a social media strategy that works
- Building a presence on social media
- Learning how to use Twitter effectively
- Building a profile on Facebook
- Build my LinkedIn profile to connect with clients
- Use Twitter to attract clients
- Market my services on the internet
- Sell on the internet

Now do something!
Knowledge is potential power.
Action is real power!

What 3 actions could you take right now?

1. _____

   _____

   _____

2. _____

   _____

   _____

3. _____

   _____

   _____

Chapter 11 - How to Win Clients and Influence Lawyers

Big Firms

When I refer to a big firm I would say the top 200 law firms in the UK. These will likely be organized more as a business, often with large departments devoted to the business processes. For the coaching function these are the people you would contact.

Head of HR

This person has overall responsibility for all HR functions. Staff and management training is only part of what they do.

Head of Learning and Development

It is likely this person will have the task of selecting, purchasing and liaising with you. This is the person who could become one of your new best friends and you theirs! Remember they have a huge task to deliver. Although they do some training "in house" they mostly rely on external service providers. There is a saying that "familiarity breeds contempt" and while I would not say that lawyers and support workers in firms treat HR with contempt, let's just say that if they hear it from someone outside the firm they are more likely to believe it! I have no scientific evidence or proof just my take on things based of several years in practice, many years on the Law Society Council and listening to my colleagues and the response to "messages" from HR. They are responsible for finding good quality external trainers and once they have found someone good they look after you.

Medium Firms

These firms may also have a dedicated HR person. It is very easy to find out who is the responsible person. In addition they will also have a partner who has reasonability for retraining. The HR person will liaise with the partner. You will recall what I said about the partnership structure and the relationship between the partners (who put money into the business and who are its owners) and the corporate types who manage various aspects of the business.

Small Firms

I would describe these as having 2-10 partners. It is less likely that they will have dedicated staff with HR function. So there will be a partner with responsibility for this function.

Sole Practitioners

Most firms in England and Wales are owned by sole practitioners. They sometimes work alone from a small office with a small support team. Some of these firms will be struggling and will find it more difficult to thrive once other non-lawyer providers enter the market. Sometimes they may be the only qualified lawyer or one of a handful, yet they hire a small army of non-qualified paralegals and support staff who do the majority of the low level work. These practices usually specialize and can make a lot of money.

Barristers' Chambers

The larger sets are more likely to have some HR support. But most don't. You will have to contact the Senior Clerk in the first instance. Or you can approach individual barristers. All their details are on their chambers' websites.

Getting your Message Right

The bigger firms may ask you to write a proposal. When you write your proposal remember in a firm more than one person will read it and they probably were not party to the conversation you had with the employee.

To save you time you can download the template at www. legalgold.co.uk/resources.

Beauty Parade

You may be invited to attend a "beauty parade". This is essentially an opportunity for you to pitch your services and products to the person who is hiring. They will probably be seeing others also, so you must make an impact. Do your research and prepare as if you are preparing for a job interview. Ring up and ask questions in advance. Make sure your message is clear and bespoke for that firm.

Here are some elements to consider:

Your pitch should be:

Clear: Tell them about your company and what you do and how you do it.

Credible: Tell them about your experience and qualifications.

Problem -   Tell them about the specific problems you have identified.

Solution - Then tell them about your proposed solutions.

Invite them to ask questions.

Conclude

Ask for the work. One of my mentors told me to ask at least six times for exactly what you want. Try this. Remember in this context "no" does not always mean "no". It could mean "not right now". Stay strong and focused.

After you have sent your email or after the beauty parade if you do not hear from them, remind them that you are there. Send them articles you have written to keep demonstrating your expertise.

If it Goes Wrong

In the six years that I have been working with lawyers I have only had one complaint. Well it wasn't actually a complaint it was a "letter before action". Even though the client had had the benefit of my time and expertise because he did not get the result he wanted the decided he wanted his money back so I promptly returned his money. I learned from the "feedback" he gave me in his letter. The point is that because they are lawyers their first instinct might be to threaten to sue you. So just make sure you have insurance and that you always have funds to make a prompt refund.

Lawyers can be challenging and they may engage in "one-up manship"

They are used to giving, not receiving advice. Just be firm - be sure about yourself and your product or service and remember to use an agreement to management expectations. Finally, use a client care letter and be very transparent on your fees so there is no "wriggle room".

Have a laugh

Lawyer: "Can you describe the individual?"

Witness: "He was about medium height and had a beard."

Lawyer: "Was this a male, or a female?"

and another...

Lawyer: "Is your appearance here this morning pursuant to a deposition notice which I sent to your attorney?"

Witness: "No, this is how I dress when I go to work."

Help me if you can

- Presentation skills
- Public Speaking
- Professional speaking
- Beauty parades
- Communication skills
- To prevent emotional stress
- Increase Energy
- Benefits of and how to cleanse your intestine and colon
- Alternative health - homeopathy
- Reiki healing
- Stress relief
- Stress prevention strategies

Now do something!
Knowledge is potential power.
Action is real power!

What 3 actions could you take right now?

1. _____

_____

_____

2. _____

_____

_____

3. _____

_____

_____

Chapter 12 -The Motherlode - How to Win Business With a Big Firm

Do you want to spend your time on just one or two clients a year? Consider the pros and cons of this. If you are wondering what it really takes to win a contract with a big firm then read on. Do you ever dream of the day when your client list includes firms like Clifford Chance, Freshfields, Norton Rose, White and Case? If you've attempted to break into that type of market you will know how difficult it can be.

It can also be intimidating. These firms are so huge that you may not even know where to start. You might even be wondering why they'd ever want to do business with your small, no-name firm. But big firms can be virtual gold mines for small businesses. If they like your product or service, they'll eagerly expand their relationship with you. But that can seem like an impossibility when you're still on the outside looking in.

Let's face it. Selling to big firms can be difficult. When you look up at their big tall buildings and see the important looking people walking around, how do you feel? These days it's getting tougher than ever to reach and influence today's super-busy, risk-averse decision makers.

The truth is, your prospects have way too much to do, and, they're expected to accomplish it with fewer resources and in less time than ever before. That's why they don't return calls and take forever to change from the status quo. So, even when you do manage to secure a meeting, the decision-making process can take forever.

Make use of the internet

Use Google Adwords to reach your ideal clients right away. This can be cheaper than hiring a sales team.

1. Change your mindset.

    Success can be duplicated. You need to believe that you can model success. Take something that exists and model how that is done. When you explain this it is such basic common sense. Less than 1% have hit the target. If we find out how they do what they do and duplicate what they do we will get the same. Tear yourself from the frustration and focus on successful people and model them. Their marketing behavior, sales psychology and their mindset. Duplicate what they did. You will get the same results or better. Otherwise we are caught up in nonsense. Ignore the media. Don't believe the press.

2. Strategy

    The sales people who earn 7 figure sums have a radically different strategy. They follow up relentlessly with customer 5, 10, 15, 20 time in ongoing sequences to get the sale.

    Use internet marketing and advertising - pay per click. Purchase Google ad words.

    You will need to make a shift in your thinking. Most people, when they look for inspiration, they look around them. But people around you are also struggling. You don't want their results, do you?

    But once you 'crack the code' of selling to big companies, you'll never look back. To be effective today, you need fresh sales strategies. Here are some ideas.

    Don't copy most people's pricing.

    You need to have a radically different pricing strategy. Model the psychology of successful people; their belief around failure. Most multi millionaires have no problem with failure. Failing is an integral part of success. Failing means you are taking so much risk that you are bound to fail at something! So don't give up. Not all your attempts will be successful. If something fails, move on. Focus on success and model successful people.

3. Double your client base.

    You need to have multiple marketing methods in your business. Have a powerful referrals strategy. There are over 90 of them. This is a key ingredient. Make referrals a key part of growing your business. Ask your clients "would you be willing to recommend me to one of your family?" Compensate them for doing so. Give them vouchers or a free gift. Use yellow pages, Google pay per click. Don't limit yourself. You won't be able to double your client base if you do. Set it as an absolute goal to double your client base.

4. Pricing

    Don't charge average low pricing. Change your pricing policy. People don't buy on price. They don't necessarily buy the cheapest. If they did then everyone would be wearing the cheapest clothes and driving cheap cars. There would be no fancy restaurants. 15% of people buy on price. Most do not. Charge more than your competitor. Sell to the 85% for whom, price is not a factor. As well as your normal rates you must also have a premium pricing policy as 5-15% of your prospects will go for the most expensive option. Another 4-5 % will spend up to 10 times more than your average price.

5. Mindset and your beliefs and psychology

    Be relentless in your focus. The reason many coaches struggle is not because of the economy. As the owner of your business you must be relentless in your pursuit of growth. Know that obstacles will come up. When you are hit with pressure, if you are not relentless, you will be battered by it. The easy option is to give up and go hide. The easy option would be to say "I can't do this". It's too hard to get lawyers as clients. It would be easy to keep your business and yourself small. So you need to think big and have great dreams and encourage your clients to do the same. It won't be easy. Your willingness to be relentless is crucial.

Most successful people resolve to do things. They don't just decide. This is what gets them through. No one ever describes an easy path. The universe will test you to see how determined you are to truly have what you want. So it will throw you some challenges. You are your resolve to be successful, whatever it takes.

6. Master on and off line marketing

Are you still using your website primarily to try to sell something? That doesn't work anymore. You'll get the occasional sale. 99% of people leave. People have now trained themselves to surf the internet. So you need to shift the purpose of your website to begin a relationship with your end user. Build a strong relationship. There is a whole strategy behind this. You need an auto responder. You need to capture their email addresses. Make a strong compelling offer that gives them something for free. Use video when they land on your page. Give them a free sample or a 30 minute consultancy. If you are not doing this then you are sitting on a fortune.

Use video extensively in all your marketing. It increases responses 100% plus. To do this properly there is a methodology. Get focused on the methodology. People's attention and focus has wandered and gone off. Focus on the right thing. There are huge opportunities. Turn off negative stuff on TV. Conduct your research online instead. Create a website that builds relationship.

Become obsessed about mastering marketing. You can't just dabble in marketing anymore. You're in the marketing business. Your job is to find other human beings, in this case, lawyers and create income now and lifelong income through keeping them. You have to understand that your client's buying process has changed forever. You must become outstanding at marketing. It is important to test multiple marketing methods. This is fun. One third of your time should be spent doing this. There are always new tools coming on the market. Stay abreast of the changes.

7. Transform your use of time

    There are fundamental core differences between people who are successful and those who are not. Successful people use their time efficiently. You need to learn to leverage technology. You can set up auto responders to communicate. It is also necessary that you do pay per click. This is a good way to leverage your time to attract leads. Use your time well and check what you do every minute of the day.

Focus

May I advise you not to dabble in this system? If, after reading this book, you decide that you want to "have a go" at this business opportunity then I would advise you not to bother. As with everything in life you have to focus. You're an achiever. You've bought this book. It's a start. I implore you to stick with it. You need time to build up your confidence, and keep going. Drill a tool until you are comfortable with it. At the networking event ask to use your Elevator Pitch. End your pitch with a question. My sales coach tells me to set specific targets and track the numbers daily, weekly and monthly. Keep sending out great content to your market. Keep feeding them and hook them in. Handle objections in your sales material.

Raise your game

You have to raise your game. You will now be playing in a different league. It raises your level and it will be great for your confidence. You've learned about the power of social proof from Robert Cialdini's book "Influence". Well, when you tell people, other big firms as well as others that you work with Clifford Chance, or another big law firm they will be impressed.

You know how people look at the achievement section of your resume first. If you land a top firm as a client then there are huge benefits, not least massive cash flow. Remember, if you land the motherlode you can outsource some of the work to associates. So make sure your network includes other good qualified coaches, trainers and consultants so that you can engage them to work with you when you land the motherlode or you can add value to your client by referring them to someone who can help them. As you become a trusted advisor they will ask you to help them find other services they need. You can agree a referral fee with the other consultant.

Benefits of Working with a Big Firm

Having a big client gives you space in your calendar to be more strategic. You can take time out to work on your business. You can plan where you want your business to be in say the next 12-24 months.

It's good for the money but it also has all these other benefits. It gives you the freedom to say no to things you don't want to do. It gives you freedom to engage in philanthropic or charitable activities, perhaps you want to mentor some school children or offer your services to disadvantaged groups who can't afford to pay it.

Imagine that you now have a full diary. How does it feel saying "no" to those former clients that you no longer have to work with because you need the money. As John Maxwell said, you can now say "no to the good so you can say yes to the great ".

What Challenges will you have?

Imagine being paid £10,000 for one day of your time. This is not unrealistic in the circumstances. Some people in the coaching business get paid £25,000 a day for their wisdom. So don't let any prior perception about big firms or companies dissuade you from going for the motherlode. Remember, even the biggest deal comes down to a handshake between 2 people. People in big firms are not different to you and me. You may have worked in a big company so you will know that they have the same issues and do exactly the same things you do. They may seem like a big giant compared to you. As Anita Ruddick has said - if you think being small is not a big deal try sharing a bed with a mosquito. It only takes a small arrow to take down a big beast. Think of the story of David and Goliath.

Big firms are like big ships that turn slowly. Generally they are unable to make quick decision, like sole practitioners and law firms and chambers can. It can take days and months to close them.

Set the Stage

You will need to set the stage to create opportunities with which to build your relationships.

Start small. Small acorns become big oaks in the right environment. One conversation can lead to something great.

If you have a book or a CD then give it to them. If you have a small pocket guide then that's even better. Remember these people are time poor! This will give them a taste of what you do.

Where Will you Find People from Big Firms

They are usually in their offices from early in the morning until very late into the evening. Even people who work in HR find that they often have to work late to get everything done to the standards that are expected.

There are regular conferences throughout the year. Find out where the HR in law conference is being held. There are many IT conferences targeted at the legal profession. Every practice area of law has a group. Find these on the professional associations' website.

Search for legal events on Google. Local law societies and state bar associations have regular events and training. There will be specialist groups. For example if your product or service is targeted at women, then the Association of Women Solicitors has a group. The State Bar Associations in the US and the Bar Council also have specialist groups. You can attend their events. Some will be free, some you will have to pay to attend.

In my experience most people know at least one lawyer. Invite them for a drink and pick their brains. Find out what's current in the legal profession. Ask them what the problems are.

Social Media and Corporate Law Firms

If they are using social media at all, then they are more likely to be on LinkedIn than any of the others. However, they don't seem to be very active on there. But they will search there when they are looking for suppliers.

Find out who their suppliers, providers and other advisers are. If they are an LLP You can find out who their accountants are from their accounts at Companies House. Their reports will give you all kinds of very useful information.

Law firms spend money on recruitment, accountants, barristers, financial advisers, and PR. Big firms are very fond of funding trainee solicitor events. Spend time with these people. Offer to do presentation for a specialist legal recruitment firm or for trainees. Remember these people have influence, even if they are not the purchaser of your services.

Go to the networking events. *The Lawyer* magazine is a good source of information on conferences and events. Start a conversation with a stranger. If you get the opportunity stand up and make a bold statement or ask a challenging question. I do this a lot. People always come to speak with you afterwards whether they agree with you or not!

Ask for the connection. Invite them to lunch. Buy them a coffee. Ask for the business. Remember the answer to every question you don't ask is "no".

How to Turn a Relationship into a Proposal

Always plan your next project while you're doing the current one. Ask them when their next staff meeting is. Offer them a "lunch and learn". This is where you go and speak to their people in their boardroom over lunch. Don't charge for addressing them. If it goes well then they will invite you again or ask you for more and offer paid work. I once ran a "tell me something new" program. I went to firms and taught them some cool stuff that I had been learning. I also invited some of my friends and fellow coaches and consultants, healers, feng shui specialists to do share their expertise when I did them. We talked about profiling, feng shui, different NLP tools - one each week. You can do this too. Make it fun and engaging and word will soon get around.

Then you can ask them what you can do for them going forward. They will introduce you to other parts of the organization.

Ask them what their needs are. Find people in your network to help them if you can't.

Say you can help - put an idea together - say "I'll put a few ideas in front of you". Or say "I've just put a program together can we talk about it?" Offer to do a sample. Ask them if it works whether that's something you can do together. You just want a couple of special relationships.

Ask them "What does success look like for you?" "What will it look like when finished?" "How do we measure success?" "Who else can I talk to make sure I cover all the bases?" "Give me more names to talk to then I can make sure I put together something appropriate".

Acknowledge their Concerns

It is very important to make sure you hit all the bases. They may think you're not big enough to deliver. They may have had a bad experience with a small company. But they may also have had a bad experience with a big company. Generally, they go with a big organization they believe can handle the volume and capacity. They will wonder if you can handle this. You may need to prove yourself with something small. If you bomb you might take them down with you. You want them to look good. Over deliver on all their expectations. Wow them, and they'll come back for more.

I once had a contract with a firm to train everyone in the firm. They had 4 different offices. It took me 3 months. A big training company would still only put one person, usually an outsourced associate, on the contract also.

Hot Tips

Use their language. If you know NLP, then match and mirror them to create and build rapport. Whatever terms and phrases they use, you should use as well.

Get hold of their external and internal documents, including their corporate social responsibility report and strategy. Get hold of their organizational charts; scoping document; roles and responsibilities; mission statement; strategies and plans. Ask them to send you information so you can better help them. Some of these will be on their websites, so check there first.

Ask them what success looks like for then. They want to look good with their bosses and their staff. Make what you do count towards helping the individual to reach their goals that go toward the overall organizational success.

Ask them what they will do after you have finished training them to embed the learning and any long term behavioral change. Let them know that you are committed to their success and the success of their company.

Demonstrate How What You do Improves Their Bottom Line

Offer external add-ons. Let them know you are not a one hit wonder, that you will still be available for them. Your success is determined by them being held accountable. Ask them how they will make sure that your coaching or training makes a long term impact. Hold them accountable to make the change - let them take you seriously. People don't care what you know till they know that you care. Let them know you care.

I remember when I worked in a City firm, the employees were very suspicious of consultants. We were a cynical bunch. There was a strong sense of not wanting anything to change for the better if it meant more money for the partners who it was generally accepted were overpaid and were leeching off the Associates and trainees. It was very much a "them" and "us". The consultant had to work hard to "win us over". They had to persuade us that they were neutral. So it's like walking on a tightrope. We didn't want anything to change

What to Expect

If they ask you to put together a proposal, don't spend too much time doing one. Often a one pager is all that is required. Ask them to pay you to put together a more detailed proposal. This lets you know they are serious. If you're a consultant don't give away any free consulting or solutions.

Build Dialog

Just put in some ideas initially. Sometimes just a one page is sufficient. If they pay you for a detailed proposal then it could be around 20 pages. Don't get wrapped up in a massive detailed proposal until you have confirmation that you are likely to get the business.

Confidentiality and Non-disclosure Agreements

On your own, you can probably only manage 2 corporate clients at a time to provide a high quality service. The firm may ask you to enter into a Non-disclosure or a Confidentiality Agreement. You will promise not to disclose any of the information you learn about the firm. It is likely that the firm will have their own policies and procedures which will include their terms. This is likely to be a more comprehensive. Don't offer a big firm your payment terms and conditions, or contract. But if it is important to you, change the payment terms so that you get paid half up from or staged monthly payments, whatever works for you.

Don't interfere with their set way of doing things. You have to conform and play their game.

They have to get it signed off and put agreements in place.

Lawyers are risk averse, safe and generally conservative. They like to bet on sure things. This includes their providers and suppliers. They want to tick the boxes. They are trained to anticipate what will go wrong and put in place agreements to make sure that it doesn't go wrong or if it does then it's clear what happens next.

You don't want to spend more than 100 days a year delivering your services. A good ratio is one third delivery, one third marketing and networking researching, writing new content, and the final third of your time "sharpening the sword" on self development, administration, personal care and rejuvenation.

If you decide you want to work with big firms then aim for 1 or 2 a year. You only need one good sized fish in your bucket for the year.

Writing Proposals and Strategy

Once you have put in your proposal ask them "How soon do you want to get started?" or "How quickly will you make the decision?" Tell them that your diary is filling up and you really want to make a space for them. "Let me give you a call in week if I have not heard from you". "Let me make a note to call you in 2 weeks if I don't hear from you". Get timescales agreed in advance so there is no uncertainty.

At the end of your email tell them when you will call them and that you'll keep calling back. Or say "if you want me to send a hard copy let me know" or "please confirm you have received this".

Remember to ask for the business. It can take a while to get the right decision. Once your proposal is in call them and tell them that another client is interested in taking you on but you want to give them first refusal. This creates scarcity.

Even after this they might come up with an excuse. Know when to quit. Keep other things going on at the same time. Don't put all your eggs in one basket. You will always get knocked back. Don't take it personal. They are not rejecting you. You might have the right ideas but it's the wrong time for them. Ask for a debrief. Ask them what you can do better. What gaps do they see in the offering? Why wouldn't it work?

Ask them if you can revisit in a few months. Offer to do a smaller version of the program or on a small scale.

If you've come this close then do more research and offer them something different. Keep the door open. Ask them what are your future plans and needs. If the firm has regional offices then build the regional relationship.

Build other Relationships

Find out who the influencers are. Do you know anyone else in the firm? Secretaries and other support staff are a mine of information and only too happy to share the gossip and the inside story on office politics. But don't believe everything they say, because they too have their own agenda. Don't ever negate the people lower down the ranks in the organization. They are a huge part of their organization. Find the names of the learning assistant, the trainee and the secretary and use their name when you phone. They all have influence even if they have no buying power.

Have a Niche

You can niche yourself in many ways. Here are three: what you do; how you do it; who you do it for. You can provide massive value by going deep rather than wide. So go deep into a niche. You become a specialist. Most programs only need one person to deliver it. Think big but operate small. If they ask you for something say "we could possibly do that for you" not" I". If they ask you who "we" are tell them you have a team of associates. Think bigger than you are.

1. Believe in yourself. Set a clear intention. Visualize yourself winning the business.

2. Don't be too available - say you're busy for the next 3-4 months.

3. If they ask for a meeting say "I'm sorry - my diary is full for the next month. You can go back later and say a space had opened up and ask them if they want it.

4. Beware of some big fish - a change in strategy or personality in the firm can squeeze you out.

5. Keep talking to others and keep doors open.

6. Don't charge per day - charge per person on a program
    - they will get more personalized service. Charge a sum
    for each person - because of the one to one they get
    afterwards. You can be more innovative with how you put
    your programs together.

7. Personalize your program. They just want to know that
    you are doing it just for them - talk their language. Law
    firms are competitive with other firms in their category.
    They will want to know that you are not giving your good
    stuff to their competitor. Tell them if they fill up your
    diary then you won't have time for anyone else, will you.
    Tell them you're a hired hand but that you would love to
    work with them exclusively.

8. Provide excellent service - if you mess up then you make it
    difficult for other solopreneurs and small business.

Have a laugh

Lawyer: "Doctor, how many autopsies have you performed on dead people?"

Witness: "All my autopsies are performed on dead people."

and another...

Lawyer: "And lastly, Peter, all your responses must be oral. Ok? What school do you go to?"

Witness: "Oral."

Lawyer: "How old are you?"

Witness: "Oral."

and another...

Lawyer: "She had three children, right?"

Witness: "Yes."

Lawyer: "How many were boys?"

Witness: "None."

Lawyer: "Were there any girls?"

Help me if you can.

- Develop a product creation strategy
- Create products and intellectual property

Now do something!

Knowledge is potential power.
Action is real power!

What 3 actions could you take right now?

1. _____

   _____

   _____

2. _____

   _____

   _____

3. _____

   _____

   _____

CAROLINE NEWMAN'S Raise the Bar™ Coaching/ Consulting Program

If I chose you to work with me ... in a Consulting/ Coaching Program for an entire year - focusing on multiplying your income, how much more do you think you could make over the next 12 months?

Email me at

Coaching@CarolineNewman.com

SECTION IV -
Mine The Gold

This is my method for separating the grit from the gold, the fool from the gold. So take on board the advice in this chapter. I believe in giving away my ideas and charging people only for the implementation of my ideas. If after reading this book you go ahead and implement the ideas and win business with lawyers I will be delighted. I know my colleagues are happy that I have written this book which I hope is providing the bridge between the coach and the legal profession.

Chapter 13 - Modern Mining

Marketing guru, Dan Kennedy, talks about the pyramid of influence. Essentially, the higher up the pyramid you go, the more influential you become and the more people want your services, and the more you can charge for them. Unfortunately, many coaches are stuck at the bottom level, with no differentiation and ultimately no clients!

Those who have niched themselves and have become a specialist are able to at least make a living. A smaller per cent reach the next stage and publish their own products. Now this could be books, CD's or DVD's. This activity brings you an additional ongoing income stream. It also allows you to spread your message through your products. It marks you out as the 'expert in your field' and consequently you will have clients actively seek you out just to do business with you. At this level, price becomes largely irrelevant. However, less than 1% of coaches ever reach 'celebrity' status. In this context celebrity status means instant name recognition in your chosen market. It means being recognized in your chosen field, even though the general population may not know who you are.

What you are looking for is to create brand awareness, so that if someone is looking for whatever your niche is, you are the name that pops into their mind. Once you've decided what your product will be on, it's relatively easy to create your first CD and have it on sale via a website where people can go online and pay with their credit card within an hour. You won't have to pay for any stock or design work or even have to ship it yourself!

I became a lawyer because I wanted to help people. I wanted to be a voice for the voiceless. I wanted to be an advocate. I found that the law did not give me the vehicle to make a difference. You were probably drawn to becoming a coach because, like me, you care about people and coaching gives you the opportunity to make a difference in the lives of others. You may be one of the many coaches who are getting by on minimum wage. You may be in debt. You may be wondering how you can do what you love and actually get paid for it. You want a return on the investment you have made in your personal development and training.

Well now you're a coach and you might be considering providing your services to lawyers.

If you are not yet a coach and you're reading this because you are interested in coaching then here's what you need to do.

Find a suitable coaching school. At the present time the fees for training a coach vary from $3,000 to $15,000.

Here are the benefits of being a Personal Coach. You can work 25 to 35 hours a week and still earn a significant income. You can work from home or hire a room near to your home. Rush hour traffic is nonexistent and you can dress comfortably. You get a great feeling of having contributed something positive to a world that is desperately in need of healing.

You are your own boss and are free from internal office politics. You will meet a lot of interesting people who will be happy to share their lives with you for a time. You can help them to achieve their dreams and goals and have more satisfying lives.

Personal Coaches join one of the most enjoyable groups of people in the world who would much rather help each other than compete. The life coaching profession is a very credible and accepted profession that appears to double in size almost every year.

How to Get Coaching Clients who Pay What you Are Worth

There is more than enough coaching clients to go around, in fact with all the change and stress going on in the world right now, there's never been a better time to be a coach.

People are not looking for a coach. They are looking for people who can help them to solve their problems. People don't want coaching, what they want is a result, an outcome, a feeling. They either want to move towards a goal or away from a problem.

Niche yourself into a specialist area so you can be looked at as an expert in that particular field.

Differentiate yourself and make yourself stand out with an idea or concept for your coaching business that instantly grabs attention. Make it a niche that people will understand in an instant.

It's a key concept, and more importantly, a key pain that people can connect to. They understand what it's about, they get it. You must find some way of differentiating yourself. Pick a niche. There are two easy ways to do this, you can either

a) go with your passions, hobbies, interests or relevant experience, or you can

b) go after the most lucrative markets.

If you choose a), you use the two P's. Who is the person that you're looking for and what is their pain?

If you understand what type of person is going to look for your products and services and you understand what their biggest pain is, you know where to go to look for them, to find them, and to turn them into clients. This immediately specializes you and marks you out as different from all the other generic coaches out there. You become a specialist.

If you choose b), I'll tell you right now that by far and away the most profitable niche for coaches right now is coaching small business owners. Not only are a lot of business owners in pain right now and desperate to make a change, but also being entrepreneurs they are more open to trying new things and taking risks. This includes smaller law firms and sole practitioners.

Consequently, if you know what you're doing it's relatively easy to get half a dozen small businesses each paying you a monthly retainer plus a percentage of the growth you help them create.

Whichever way you choose, you must niche, if you don't you have virtually zero chance of building a coaching business that gives you the lifestyle you want, especially in the current economy.

Have an Initial Consultation Session

I know that you may be uncomfortable with selling. So don't sell. Make the whole session a coaching session. Allow the prospect to transition into a full paying client by enrolling them.

These complimentary sessions are extremely effective if done the right way and in the right circumstances.

As a coach it is our duty to stand in front of a potential client and congruently tell them that coaching with you will absolutely, without any shadow of a doubt, get the result their after.

You want to look them square in the eye and say congruently: "I have seen this all a hundred times before, I absolutely can help you get the result you are after, work with me and I promise you'll be exceptionally happy with the results". The bottom line is, you need to learn how to be able to ethically influence and persuade others in order to effectively sell yourself as a coach. If you can't, you will always struggle to find clients.

Run your Coaching Practice as a Professional business

Now even if you are the best coach you need to learn how to market your business. Maybe you know someone who is a fantastic coach comes from a real heart space, has great ideas and even has some great products, but they have difficulty getting clients.

On the other hand can you think of a coach who is your opinion is rather average yet they somehow manage to get a lot of clients. Did you answer "yes" to these questions? So quite clearly then, it is not how good you are as a coach that determines the clients you get. How good you are determines how many clients you keep, but you need to get them first.

The way to have a successful coaching practice with longevity is to run it like a business. I want you to have a really successful business that is why I am writing this book to open up to coaches a market that you might not otherwise find it easy to access. The more of us out there helping people solve their problems in an authentic way the better it is for society.

I want you to succeed and be professional about it. Otherwise you damage the reputation of our fledgling profession. The last thing you want is for your business to go under while you are in the middle of a contract or for something to happen to you and you are unable to deliver for your clients. Here is one way for you to secure the long term future of your practice.

If you follow this advice, your coaching business will prosper where the vast majority fail. You'll never have a problem finding clients ever again. You will have an easy time filling your practice. You can relax and concentrate on delivering a high level service to your clients.

You will have the joyous, fulfilling business you dreamed of having when you left your corporate job. You can work anywhere and have a truly global business and get paid handsomely for sharing your gift and helping others to achieve their dreams.

Master the skill of marketing yourself and sharing with the world how you can help them to solve their problems. If you know how to market yourself, you can find as many clients as you want, as quickly as you want. You can charge whatever prices you want. You can fill your own seminars and workshops easily.

You can still employ the elegant enrolment conversation for those people who still want to have a conversation and get to know you before they become clients.

You can choose who you work with (just think, you can work only with the most motivated, easy to work with and best paying clients!) And you can live the life you always dreamed of.

You might be in debt or you might even have gotten into debt to pay for your coaching courses and the myriad of other personal development courses that are on the market. Now it's your time to reap the rewards of your investment. You want to help people but you also need to help yourself first. You cannot give what you don't have.

A while back I decided to stop coaching. I also used to speak at events. I decided to stop doing that also. Why? Because I felt like a fraud. I was struggling financially because I just couldn't get all the pieces of the puzzle. I had been going to seminars for years. Each time I went to seminar or bought a book or CD or DVD I learned some new cool stuff. I learned how the mind worked with Bob Proctor. I learned about authenticity at Landmark but somehow I couldn't make all this work for my business. I trained in NLP. I became a trainer. I thought to myself: "How can I coach people to have success in their lives when my life isn't working?" Perhaps you feel or have felt this way in the past. Here's the thing: you can still coach others to get to their SuccessVille even if you haven't "arrived" at yours. But it will help your confidence if you are on your way, if you have clarity, if you are not burdened with debt you don't know how to pay. So take care of yourself first.

Here is a tried and tested formula for attracting prospects using the power of the internet promoted by Dan Kennedy and other internet marketing specialists. It involves using the internet to market yourself as an expert. It is one of the ways to attract prospects. There are many courses on internet marketing and there are other things you can do. For example using Google adwords to find the key words that your niche market is searching for.

Create Products

So now you have chosen your niche. Create some products that you can give away on the internet. You can hire people to create the products for you. Then you can hire them to create systems that will send you new leads every week.

There are just 3 things you need to do...

1. Create something of value that when people see/hear it, it will naturally spark their interest in your coaching. At its most basic level, you can create a free report.

2. Design a series of emails or a free mp3 recording. It needs to be short, to the point and give some great information.

If you wish to record something, buy a cheap microphone that will plug into your PC or Mac, there's tons of free recording software out there. Record 30 minutes of great information that will be relevant for your chosen niche market.

3. Go to www.elance.com (it's an online market place for freelance web programmers, designers, writers, etc) and post a job asking for someone to take your free report and 'spruce it up', add graphics and convert into a pdf.

    You could also ask someone to write/rewrite the report for you to make it more powerful and easier to read. It's free to post a job and then the potential providers will 'bid' to do your work. You can check out their work and feedback and then pick the provider who's a combination of the best price and best quality. You can expect to pay around $50, and within 72 hours you'll have a fantastic free product to give away!

    Go back to Elance and post a second job, asking for a web programmer to build you a basic two page website, explain that you need to capture people's emails (and phone numbers if you want to phone them) and send them your free gift when they sign up. For between $100-$200, your site will be up and running within a week! The experienced programmers on Elance will let you know if they need anything else from you and answer any of your questions. The only other thing you will want to do is write the email that the person gets with the freebie to encourage them to contact you for coaching.

For example:

Dear <FIRST NAME>

Thank you for downloading my free report "How to lose weight without dieting", you can download it here: <LINK>

In it you will find lots of useful information to get you started.

However, if you would like to get moving quicker, I specialize in taking people from square one, all the way within 3 months through 1-1 mentoring. If you'd like to know more about this, please contact me on

<INSERT CONTACT INFO>

Please note, I can only work with a maximum of 10 clients at any one time to maintain quality. I currently have 7 so I have space for a further 3 clients, so please get in touch asap if you're serious about losing weight without dieting.

Yours

<YOUR NAME>

This is a brief example. Now you've got a website that you can direct people to that will automatically funnel much more highly qualified clients in your direction. Clearly, there are many, many options for you to take the above system to the next level (e.g. sending them multiple emails over a set amount of days via an autoresponder, selling them products and so forth.)

The only point you need to understand is once you've set up your system, you'll never have to worry about wasting your time with free sessions that don't go anywhere or in fact have to find your own clients ever again!

101 LIQUID GOLD 21ST MARKETING TIPS

This book cannot go into all the details about marketing. There are lots of books and websites that will help you with this. I have given you a taster. But I have collated this checklist to help you stay focused and to attract lawyer prospects to your pipeline, quickly and consistently.

The key is to slowly and systematically add these marketing methods to the way you market yourself. You'll get results in time. So get your prospecting pan out and start today.

1. Know your value and your true worth. Keep reminding yourself that you have great value to offer.

2. Come from a Full Practice Mentality. Believe that you already have lots of clients, even if you currently don't. You won't appear desperate to make a sale.

3. Follow up with all prospects in less than 48 hours.

4. Define your ideal client very specifically.

5. Have a clear proposition and declare this on your website, your LinkedIn or other Social media sites and your business card.

6. Write out your Unique Selling Proposition and practice it often. Pin it up on your walls in your office and your home. Include brief details of the problem you help solve.

7. Write out what separates you from your competition. I personally don't believe in competition. There is plenty for everyone. I focus more on being creative.

8. Craft and memorize your elevator speech.

9. Join select networking groups but have a clear strategy.

10. Start doing your own workshops.

11. Get hired for speaking engagements.

12. Have a Client Attractive business card that gets you business. This has to be of good quality. No free vistaprint cards!

13. Create a website that excites prospects - make it clear and relevant. Focus on benefits.

14. Ask for referrals. Educate and nurture your clients and contacts. Ask for the referral and reward them for helping you out.

15. Give clients birthday gifts.

16. Always add extra value.

17. Have a niche and be a specialist.

18. Decide the lifestyle you want and the number of hours you want to work.

19. Cluster your client appointments to make time for your marketing.

20. Get clear on where your best clients have come from.

21. Don't be a secret; get out there and let people know about the gift you bring to the world.

22. Focus on your top 5 or 10 clients for referrals.

23. Don't ever discount.

24. Take the edge off by offering a guarantee.

25. Use technology to get clients while you sleep.

26. Keep a Warm Prospects List for easy follow up.

27. Don't be needy for clients (keep your day job or work part-time if you need to or be an Associate with someone else's company until you build your own business).

28. Educate your environment with a fun introduction letter.

29. Ask personal advocates for referrals.

30. Think about and communicate what a GOOD lead for you is.

31. Communicate what a BAD lead for you is.

32. Talk about benefits and results, not features!

33. Set up incentives for referrals.

34. Get testimonials from your raving fans.

35. Raise your rates.

36. Get a really good marketing and business coach.

37. Don't sell: show how you solve problems and add value.

38. FOCUS: a strong focus now creates a different future later.

39. Ask clients for measurable and tangible results in their goals.

40. Tell everyone what you do and what problems you help people to solve.

41. Create strategic alliances and joint ventures. Nurture these relationships.

42. Make clients feel special - offer free samples, discounts, other exclusive services.

43. Strive for a 100% referral based practice.

44. Reward people for sending referrals.

45. Do regular mailings/postcards.

46. Set up your office for efficiency. Use the strategies in this book.

47. Become a professional.

48. Believe in yourself - write down why you're really good at what you do.

49. Invest in your personal and professional development.

50. Get a personal board of directors - create or join a mastermind team.

51. Put your expertise on paper and sell it (people love information).

52. Strengthen your strengths by delegating.

53. Use buzz words instead of long sentences.

54. Don't make a prospect wrong if they don't sign up. Remember you have been of service just by letting them know you are available to help them.

55. Write and publish a book.

56. Get on boards, get involved in community, and be visible.

57. Create a signature talk you're known for.

58. Collect names religiously.

59. Use a database management system.

60. Create an idea book so you can focus on 2 or 3 things max.

61. Walk your talk - make sure you're using your own information or product.

62. Use client case studies in sales conversations.

63. Surround yourself with supporters and positive people who bring out the best of who you are.

64. Prioritize - work only on things that make money from 9 till 5 pm.

65. Celebrate your Wins - don't take them for granted.

66. Create online programs and hold teleseminars and free webinars

67. Ask for feedback and suggestions from top clients.

68. Create a one-sheet flyer or brochure.

69. Work with groups for more income.

70. Do research on new targets and their critical needs.

71. Become an expert in your field.

72. Position yourself as a problem solver.

73. Be a "connector" - connect people together.

74. Brand yourself big time and brand all your product offerings.

75. Create intellectual property in your business.

76. Host a club or association in your industry.

77. Write a newspaper column.

78. Use your email signature as a Client Attraction tool.

79. Host a special interest group.

80. Spend extra time with your best clients.

81. Have a marketing plan in place vs. doing things ad hoc.

82. Get a professional logo.

83. Seek out and get to know good networkers.

84. Accept credit cards.

85. Host brainstorming sessions with clients.

86. Write 3 handwritten thank you notes per day.

87. Do 5 lunches, breakfasts, and coffees per week to spread the word.

88. Have all the necessary business equipment.

89. Make a list of organizations that need speakers.

90. Launch a party for your business.

91. Create programs rather than onetime sessions.

92. Keep your materials simple - less is more.

93. Set up 3 short term goals per month.

94. Communicate what you do as if they're 6 years old.

95. Create a list of your credibility factors.

96. List the best ways to easily and inexpensively reach ideal clients.

97. Figure out what image you must have to make your target audience want to work with you.

98. Write newsletters for associations of which you are a member.

99. Have a list of speech topics ready to go.

100. Be known for one thing.

101. Provide a diamond service to your clients.

Chapter 14 - Is Your Net Working?

Now you have learned how to get the attention of lawyers, it is important to make an impression that helps you seal the deal. The following information and advice will help you learn how to seal the deal with a lawyer once they are interested in your service.

Many lawyers are naturally curious and interested in meeting someone who has a different perspective on their profession: this is beneficial to them as it helps them learn how their potential clients view them and how they can use this as an advantage. The best way to convert a lawyer's interest in your service to actually purchasing it is to build a network where you can engage in this curiosity, by building a relationship with them. After all, anyone would be more comfortable working with someone they already know than with a complete stranger.

Before you start networking however, you need to know why you are doing this. Networking is a great way to increase business. If you already have some clients, but are looking for a larger client base, it is one of the best ways to enhance your business since it allows your client to get a real feel of how you work, what services you provide, and how they can benefit from your input into their work and lives.

Now, you must learn a few things about networking. The first step to building a powerful network is to be bold! You don't have the time to blunder about shooting everything in range, but you have time for one precise shot, and it must be right on target.

When face-to-face, you need a short, clear and easy statement to describe what you offer in your services; this effective statement is known as an "elevator pitch".

There are simple rules for elevator pitch delivery:

Your tone must be compelling and you must be enthusiastic about the product you are pitching; don't be nervous or fidgety as this will make the person think that you are not confident about the product you are pitching.

Don't use technical jargon that the person wouldn't understand; the person must feel confident in their understanding of the pitch you are delivering, and clear about what you are saying.

When you attend networking events, have a networking strategy. Remember to try your best to make a positive impression - dress professionally, and act like you would in a meeting. If you're going to a lawyer event then a suit or a smart dress is appropriate. You want to have instant rapport with them. Showcase your passion and remember to be in a good frame of mind.

1. Write down one way to take a conversation with a potential client from 'interested' to free initial session, arrange a meeting, or whatever your outcome would be.

2. Plan out exactly how it would go in your mind.

3. Next, mentally rehearse this scenario over and over and over until you have it clearly in your mind.

    Finally, go to your next potential networking meeting and use this one introduction to engage 10 potential clients. The next day, sit down again for a few minutes and think about how it worked for you. Think about ways you could improve your approach, and if you come up with some good innovations, go ahead and do the same process of mentally rehearsing the new ideas until you have them down.

Rehearse scenarios with your potential clients. You need one good, solid, default thing to do in each common situation with potential clients. So pick one, and refine it until your mind no longer goes blank!

If you are trying to build a network, I recommend that you regularly check Lawdacity's website for new opportunities to meet lawyers and their colleagues.

Choosing to have a positive mindset while developing your network is really important because it will influence how you act during your pitch delivery. Thinking positive enables you to be more confident and helps prevent any anxiety that may try to attack you.

The problem is most coaches go to business networking meetings without a specific objective in mind. Then if by luck somebody expresses an interest in coaching, your mind goes blank and you end up having a very generic discussion about coaching, rather than if you can help them and making them a client. How do you overcome this?

One of the concepts that I teach is "Have one good default thing to do in common situations". In other words, it sounds to me like you just haven't taken the time to work out a basic system for yourself that will allow you to naturally engage and convert potential clients you come across in one of these situations.

Have a laugh

Lawyer: "Are you married?"

Witness: "No, I'm divorced."

Lawyer: "And what did your husband do before you divorced him?"

Witness: "A lot of things I didn't know about."

and another...

Lawyer: "How did you happen to go to Dr. Casey?"

Witness: "Well, a lady down the road had several of her children by Dr. Casey and said he was really good."

and another...

Lawyer: "Were you acquainted with the deceased?"

Witness: "Yes sir."

Lawyer: "Before or after he died?"

Help me with these

- Build and develop my network

- Cultivate my network

- Get a Return on my Investment from Networking

- Get recommendations and referrals

- Who to include my network

Now do something!
Knowledge is potential power.
Action is real power!

What 3 actions could you take right now?

1. _____

_____

_____

2. _____

_____

_____

3. _____

_____

_____

Chapter 15 - Easy Selling

If the 49ers were around today they wouldn't be panning for gold in the streams of California. They would be mining for treasures on the internet and on Social Media Sites.

The old miners had to prospect or try to target based on these 3 things - knowing certain rocks were where gold was to be found; having hunches on where to look and just seeking luck.

Modern miners have the advantage of technology - scanners, computer programs to work out likelihood, drills to gather samples and they have machinery to excavate in no time.

The internet and social media has given us modern advantages for businesses seeking to mine gold. Computers allow ease of being a small operation due to software innovations and having an office on the hoof; connections to the world and clients via internet technology and social media; research about lawyer clients and how to connect with them.

Lawyers are more available via the new technology for those who have smart phones. can be reached when out of the office. Coaches can now support their clients virtually even when they are normally "unavailable". Technology has broken down contact and connection boundaries. Social media gives coaches the opportunity to reach lawyers who are becoming more involved in social media, albeit tentatively in most cases.

The Attraction of Law

How do you become attractive to the legal professional so that they will hire you? The market is crowded but there are very few people and companies who specialize in coaching and training lawyers.

You may be asking: "How can you compete with the big training companies?" Well, you develop a deep knowledge of your subject and of your target market. By reading this book you will now have more knowledge about the legal profession than many others.

Be confident that you are the "go to" choice in what you do.

Dealing with Business and Competition

Let's face it; we're not in the most financially stable times right now. There is competitiveness in every area of the market, not just in coaching practice. And, this is particularly challenging for the coaches because most of you aren't trained to be business people. How do they deal with price competition when someone else will offer the same services that you do at a quarter of your rate?

According to the laws of marketing: the only way you can convince your customer that you deserve to be paid four times the competition (see above) is to completely stand out from the crowd. That is where coaches can excel at bolstering your ability to run your businesses by enabling you to build your business, brand and service strategies.

You can to set yourself apart from the crowd and ensure your clients know that you are the best option available. Your goal as a coach is to develop an efficient business so that you can earn a profit.

Dealing with the Problem of Selling

I know that most of you, like most lawyers, simply do not like to. But you know that you have to do it to survive. The reasons why lawyers think that they shouldn't or couldn't sell their services include: lack of time; believing that they're above selling their services; believing that selling is "dirty"; believing that lawyers should only handle law and leave the rest to someone else. What are your reasons? Interestingly, some coaches also have this problem. You know that you have value to add to someone's life, that you can help them to achieve their goals, yet you find it hard to sell.

As with lawyers you have to put your service out there, make it stand out from the crowd and be prepared to deal with interested prospects. This is the only way that you can attract clients in this type of economy.

If you choose to ignore this message now, I have news for you; while times may be tough now, they're going to get tougher. Competition increases every moment, and if you don't know how to attract clients then there's no chance of you succeeding. Coaching is an industry, and you have to behave in that way.

Sell to Lawyers

It is not hard to sell to lawyers. You can gain these sales once you become a confident at selling.

I've given you an overview of the international legal profession and the legal market. I've introduced you to the various parts of the legal profession and the different types of lawyers and what drives them. I've reminded you of the great value that you can offer to people who want your help. Remember, by the time people come to you for coaching they are either curious or they feel defeated.

In this chapter I'm going to show you my sales process. This is the process that I have used to get clients in the legal market.

First you find your prospects. Do this by acquiring and growing your list of people in your target market. This can be through social media, networking meetings or direct mail.

Write down and practice your pitch until you are pitch perfect. Then call your prospect and follow up with them. Use a sales script. The coaching begins here. Ask them about themselves. What are their goals? What's stopped them from achieving their goals? The aim of this call is to introduce them to coaching and your particular style of coaching by offering them a complimentary coaching session. Agree a date for the complimentary session. Set them some homework. Ask them to think about what goal they want to achieve. Email them the form for them to complete.

The Complimentary Session

Then hold your complimentary session. This can all take place over the phone or in person. It should last 40 minutes. Build rapport with the client, even if it's over the phone. Once someone has agreed to have a complimentary session they probably want coaching. Think about the session and prepare as if you have been coaching this person for a year. You'll be far more prepared to deal with objections you might get at the end. It is very important that you master the complimentary session. You will find that if there are any objections at the end they will not be as strong and it will be easy for you to handle them.

I cannot, of course, explain to you how to overcome every single objection in all the ways they can be presented, in this book. But I will show you how to handle some of the more common ones. The three reasons for you to do the complimentary session are to provide value, to share your excitement at introducing them to coaching to give them a taste of coaching. The second reason is to determine if coaching can work for them so they can make a decision. The third reason is for you to decide whether you want them as a client. You should be interviewing them. You want to find out if you have rapport and if in fact you are the best coach for them.

If you don't already do complimentary sessions then you ought to consider doing some. Be professional about it and this will prove to be beneficial for you later.

It is very important that you follow the structure. The complimentary session should only be marketed to your target market and your niche: the exact people you are looking for and the exact people that want what you have. The more congruent they are the better. You don't just wasn't anybody and everybody. You don't want to be all things to all people. The more focused you are on who you want to coach and what you want to coach them on the better. This will enable you to see the benefit of this. If you give 20 complimentary sessions you ought to close 15 clients. These prospects are now highly qualified.

You will do marketing only to secure complimentary sessions. Direct mail, networking, advert, website, speaking. You are looking to sell a complimentary session. All you are looking to do is to add value.

This will build your confidence level. Do 20 complimentary sessions a month? You will get more clients. It's a numbers game.

We are coaches. We want to coach and provide value. It's easier to sell a complimentary session than to try to secure them as a client. Give them a great experience of you and your coaching style. Tell them that at the end of the session you will be asking them to take you on as their coach.

The most Common Objections and How to Deal With Them

I have found that there are six main objections. Here they are:

"I need to think about it for a little bit". "I just don't have the time". "I'm not sure if coaching is right for me" "I need to check with my husband/wife/business partner"; "I'd like to talk to some other coaches before I make up my mind" and the final one "That's way too much money I don't think I can afford it".

Remember you're not looking for friends. You are here to challenge the prospect. As you go through the session and ask for the business you might detect physical changes. Observe their body language and physiology. Hold them accountable for the goals they have said they want to achieve and have not achieved so far.

How to Overcome these Objections

In this process, there are four components to overcoming objections.

1. Lay the foundation

    Let the prospective client know at the beginning of the complimentary session that at the end you will be asking them if they would like to hire you to be their coach. The prospective client is probably wondering when they are going to get the sales' pitch. They know what it's about. It's to provide them with value and to determine if coaching will work for them. They know you are going to try and sell them. Take the honest approach. This builds trust and takes their fear away. They and you can then just focus on the coaching session.

    At the start of the call say: "Sarah, thank you for calling me today for this complimentary session". I'm very excited to show you the value that coaching can bring to your life. Did you get a chance to do that homework? Sarah, let me take a little time to show you how the next 40 minutes will work. The first thing I'm going to do is share with you a little bit about the coaching profession. If I remember correctly you don't know much about it, do you? This is your opportunity to get the benefit of some coaching.

You'll do most of the talking. It is my goal that you will receive great value from the session whether you decide to hire me or not. At the end I shall share with you a little of how my coaching practice works and what my fees are. I'm going to ask you if you'd like to hire me to be your coach. Is that ok?"

The big thing you are doing is establishing a level of trust. But you are also tricking yourself into asking them for the sale. It's important that you do this at the end. Don't be fearful. You've already told them at the beginning that you are going to ask them.

That foundational step of letting them know in the beginning that you're going to ask them is so critical.

2. Prepare your mind to receive an objection and handle it effectively. This is the pre-objection phase. Set the intention that the prospect will choose you to be their coach. But at the same time be prepared for objections and hold the vision of how you have successfully handled it. You are going to get concerns, questions and objections. Some will be true objections. Some will be more questions. I have found that only 10% of prospects actually hire the coach on the spot, without the benefit of a complimentary session. The other 9 out of 10 will have objections. Don't think less of yourself. Know they are coming and prepare for them.

3. Practice. It takes practice to handle objections effectively. By practicing you will raise your skill level and your confidence so that you can overcome any objections. There is a six step preparation process.

    i. Practice in your mind and get clear how you'll overcome every objection.

    ii. Then practice it in front of the mirror. Talk to yourself. What will I say if someone says this? Know the objections are coming.

iii. Practice in front of your cat or dog. Once you've mastered it in the mirror.

iv. Practice with another coach. Ask them to give you feedback.

v. Practice with a friend who is not a coach. Say to them: "one of the ways I am building my coaching practice is through complimentary sessions. I may get some objections. Would you mind practicing with me so that I am prepared"?

vi. Bring it to the public.

4. Work on building the belief you have in yourself. Get your level of belief in your ability to a high level. In our live event we have fun getting your belief to such a level that when someone gives you an objection you almost find it silly. You are so confident in your ability help them. You have to believe that we belong to an amazing profession. You will respond in a completely different way. Imagine your belief in yourself being 10 times higher than it is now. How you will respond to objections will be very different. You will feel powerful. You will be attractive and that is what people want. Anything you can do to build your belief in yourself that will be the greatest time you can spend. When you get that level of belief your practice will skyrocket. You can then respond powerfully to anyone who gives you an objection.

The next component is a beautiful, simple technique. It will enable you to close the sale. The one line to say to virtually every objection you hear.

"Caroline, that sounded really good but it's just too expensive…"

You say: "Well Simon I appreciate that. As I mentioned earlier I wasn't going to hard sell you or pressure you in any way and I want to honor that. I can let you go right now, or if you like, we can talk about this. Which would you prefer?"

Ninety five percent of people will say: "I want to talk about it". This is particularly true if you have followed the structure and delivery of the complimentary session.

The complimentary session should be fun and energetic. Use it to build trust and explain exactly how you can help them. When you have done the complimentary session and you get an objection you have two choices. The answer is simple. They want to get coached. That's why they are here. They want you to overcome their objection. So when you establish that level of trust you have their permission to handle their objection.

I've had many people say: "what do you mean, let me go". They will say: "I want to talk about it". They'll almost feel insulted or hurt that you're talking about letting them go. You have given them a taste of how you can help them to reach their goals and dreams, now they're giving you an objection and you are telling them you might take away their goal and dream!

This isn't about manipulation. It's about believing in yourself as a coach and how you can help them and not being bashful. Your job is to get them to a level where they believe it too.

Have fun with it and be yourself. Once they say they want to talk about it, you continue coaching them. That's the mindset you want to have throughout the process. If you use this methodology then it will work for you. Remember to be congruent with who you are.

If they say money is too tight then you start being a coach. Say to yourself: "what would I say to this person if I've been coaching them for a year?" "How would I be if they were already my client?" Say whatever comes to your mind. Remember you have rapport with them and you have established a level of trust. This will give you a high level of confidence. You will be able to say something you might not normally be able to say. They will react favorably. It will lay the proper foundation for what coaching is all about.

You will find mp3s containing role plays on the website. www. legalgold.co.uk

Have a laugh

Lawyer: "Mr. Smith, you went on a rather elaborate honeymoon, didn't you?"

Witness: "I went to Europe, sir."

Lawyer: "And you took your new wife?"

and another...

Lawyer: "I show you Exhibit 3 and ask you if you recognize that picture."

Witness: "That's me."

Lawyer: "Were you present when that picture was taken?"

Help me if you can

- Read quicker and still retain information

- Improve my memory

Now do something!
Knowledge is potential power.
Action is real power!

What 3 actions could you take right now?

1. _____

   _____

   _____

2. _____

   _____

   _____

3. _____

   _____

   _____

Chapter 16 - Don't Let Them Scare You

When you go to meetings with clients and prospects you prepare. If you didn't you'd feel nervous, vulnerable, anxious and exposed...the list goes on. When you attend business related events you are going to meet potential prospects, maybe existing clients and contacts.

Consider some of these planning points:

*   Who's going to be there? Know who's going to be there so you can be suitably prepared and dressed.

*   Do some research on the people and the type of occasion, act accordingly.

*   Ascertain the format; know whether the event you're attending is formal or casual.

*   Know the timings. Being late never sets a good impression!

*   Know the event location. This means you know how long you need to get there.

*   Knowing the event dress code; dress appropriately!

*   What to talk about. While it's hard to prepare conversations before hand, have some topics ready so that if need be, you have something to fall back on.

*   Ensure you ask someone to repeat their name when you don't hear it; they'll never say "I told you once; I'm not going to tell you again!"

Now that you know how to improve your networking skills, the next chapter will help you learn how to deal with a somewhat common problem which you could face while networking. Don't let rude networkers spoil your evening.

Don't be put off by a lawyer who might at first appear to be arrogant. This is the rude, disrespectful ignorant networker; he generally attends events and he generally upsets lots of people. What does he do to create this unhappy situation? Also be aware that when you attend an event you find that everyone seems to know everyone else but you don't know anyone? What do you do? Be prepared. Research the current hot topics so that you can contribute sensibly to conversations.

Here are 10 behaviors to be aware of and avoid or counter:

1. He doesn't understand the rules of space. He stands too close and for those with claustrophobia this is a living hell. Even if you take a step back, he follows and closes the space that you just made.

2. He comes over to you whilst you're chatting with someone else. He knows that person, but not you. While he takes the time to acknowledge and greet the person he knows, he completely ignores you, without even saying hello.

3. If three of four people are talking, he completely ignores you and proceeds to chat with the other people of the group, leaving you to stand by yourself.

4. When he gets bored, he simply walks off. He does not bother to state that he's going to leave, and doesn't even have the consideration to make an excuse.

5. He constantly hijacks the conversation. "Oh I've been there. I know someone better than him. I can beat that, it only took me..." He's always got a story to top the one that's being discussed at the moment, and does not even bother to make apologies for interrupting.

6. He is downright rude. He does not make considerations for the feelings of other people, makes snide or rude comments about other people, their businesses, personal lives etc. Apparently, there is nothing off bounds for him.

7. He interrupts conversations which are obviously meant to be private. He does not consider the fact that certain people might like to keep certain information private, but tries to take part in conversations which have nothing to do with him.

8. He drinks too much too soon, or doesn't know how to handle his alcohol. He behaves like the typical drunk, and doesn't make considerations for the type of people that he is surrounded by.

9. He tells inappropriate jokes or anecdotes. He does not show respect for the people that are around him, and makes offensive and inappropriate comments.

10. Then there's the person who looks over your shoulder or around the room as he's talking to you. His body language is saying "I'm bored with you Will, I want out of here". Fine, you don't want to build a relationship with this hooligan do you? Move on. Simply say "Well, it's good to meet you chief hooligan, will you excuse me I need to see my friend May over there". He'll think "Thank goodness for that!"

However, it is important to remember that this rude networker should not be allowed to ruin everything! Most lawyers are incredibly professional, and very unlike this rude networker. So if you meet this type of behavior, remember that it is best to move forward and attract other people. Ask someone to introduce you. I have learnt to have fun at these events. People are always curious about what I do and they will be curious about you too. So be interesting and have your pitch ready.

I have read a variety of books about networking. I have come to realise that there are essentially two types of networking and therefore two different approaches.

The first type of event is where you meet people that you will see all the time, such as a regular networking event, or breakfast meeting. Here the strategy is to build deep relationships. You are likely to meet people for one to ones.

The second type of event is where you may not meet that person again unless you go out of your way to develop the relationship. At these events I will ask the person about themselves and listen to them. Then when they ask me I use my elevator pitch and ask the person directly if that is something that interests them. If they say "yes" then I tell them more about what I do. If they say "no" then I ask them if they know someone who might be interested in my services. If he says "yes" then I offer him my card to pass on to that person. At these events, usually conferences, I treat it as a numbers game and I will work the room like a butterfly.

Have a laugh

Lawyer: "Were you present in court this morning when you were sworn in?"

and another...

Lawyer: "Do you know how far pregnant you are now?"

Witness: "I'll be three months on November 8."

Lawyer: "Apparently, then, the date of conception was August 8?"

Witness: "Yes."

Lawyer: "What were you doing at that time?"

and another...

Lawyer: "How many times have you committed suicide?"

Witness: "Four times."

Help me if you can

- Find an outsourced PA

- Get the best out of outsourcing

- Manage my risk with outsourcing

- Honor my compliance obligations

Now do something!
Knowledge is potential power.
Action is real power!

What 3 actions could you take right now?

1. _____

   _____

   _____

2. _____

   _____

   _____

3. _____

   _____

   _____

SECTION V -
Become A Pro

Once a gold miner had successfully located and mined gold, he was rich beyond his dreams! Wait, was he really?

While he did know where to get gold, would anyone really buy the unrefined gold that is found in mines? No. So in order to make a profit, the miners had to get their gold refined into products that were worth something; gold bars, gold flakes, jewelry etc.

Then the miners usually bought a ranch or a house with the money that they made - turning their gold into profit even when it wasn't directly involved in helping the business grow.

Chapter 17 - Develop a Professional Coaching Business

Now that you have learned how to mine, where to mine, what tools to use, and how to maintain productivity, it is necessary that you know what you're going to do with the gold once you've mined it. Just having access to gold won't alone make you profitable, but using the gold, refining it and investing it will give you not only current profit but profit for years to come.

Once a miner was rich, his social standing improved considerably. Since this was a time of perceived nobility, a miner had to change his personality if he wanted to fit in with the new society that surrounded him.

No longer could he be the brash, unkempt person that he was before. Now he must act civilized, cultured, and be constantly well mannered. This would lead to him being accepted into his new social surroundings.

Much like the miner, you must now be more of a professional; lawyers are members of a profession and they want to see this reflected in their coaching and training company. I believe that eventually coaching companies will become more professional. Certainly the International Coaching Federation is working towards establishing itself as the regulator of the profession. So you can choose to manage your business more professionally.

Working with Associates

If you decide to work with a big firm and engage Associates to work with you then you might want to consider having some structures and policies in place. Here are some policies and forms you might want to consider. This is one quarter of the policies, forms and documents that law firms are required to have in place to comply with the Regulations. You might choose to compile this as an office manual. This is important for you to protect your business reputation and brand. Any Associates that you engage will be made aware of the standards you adhere to in your professional coaching practice. If you let your prospects know that you have this manual then they will probably be more inclined to work with you. You can take your time to do this. This could be your next step towards making your business more professional.

Set up Systems

Your manual could contain the following documents:

The legal status of the business (LLC, LLP, Limited Company, Sole Trader)

The Company's commitment to quality

Avoiding discrimination and achieving diversity

Health and safety

Planning

My Business and marketing plan

Business continuity - how will you continue to serve your clients in the event of emergencies?

Financial management

Computer systems

Management reports

Income and expenditure budgets

Cashflow

Receipts of cash and cheques

Receipts for cheques and cash

Cheque requisitions

Transfers

Write-offs

Petty cash

Issue of bills and cheques

ICT and facilities

Information management

Management of the IT system

Data protection

Information management

E-mail policy

The client appointment procedure

Telephone calls

Post and communications

Incoming mail

Outgoing mail

Health and safety

Health and safety at work

Supervision and risk management

Supervision

Systems of supervision

Work allocation

Maintaining progress

File reviews

Managing risk

Reporting risk

Risk review

Client care

Policy on client care

Dress and demeanour

Client confidentiality

Associate's responsibilities

Complaints handling

Client surveys

Case and file management

Preliminary issues

Client enquiries

Accepting a new Client

Situations where coachee request must be declined

File opening

Conflict of interest

Costs and payments information

File maintenance

File summary sheets

Attendance notes

Confidentiality

Closing a Client's File

File closing

Final review

Archiving

FORMS

File opening form - how your associates could open a client file.
A checklist of things they might do

Client care letter

Terms and conditions

Complaints procedures

Client complaint report form

Client complaints register

Client survey form

Associate Feedback form

Training feedback form

Have a laugh

Lawyer: "You don't know what it was, and you didn't know what it looked like, but can you describe it?"

and another...

Lawyer: "You say that the stairs went down to the basement?"

Witness: "Yes."

Lawyer: "And these stairs, did they go up also?"

and another....

Lawyer: "Have you lived in this town all your life?"

Witness: "Not yet."

Now do something!
Knowledge is potential power.
Action is real power!

What 3 actions could you take right now?

1. _____

_____

_____

2. _____

_____

_____

3. _____

_____

_____

Chapter 18 - Continuous Professional Development / Continuing Legal Education

In England and Wales the Continuing Professional Development year runs from November 1 to October 31. CPD credits are given for approved activities which include: participation in accredited or non-accredited courses, coaching and mentoring sessions, writing on law or practice, work shadowing, producing a dissertation, studying towards a professional qualification.

The previous chapter listed some of the common problems lawyers face; the following section will help you understand how your services dovetail neatly in with a compulsory requirement they must complete each year...

CPD is Regulated - no CPD no Practicing License

The Continuing Professional Development (CPD) scheme is dictated by the Solicitors Regulation Authority. All solicitors and registered European lawyers (RELs) in legal practice or employment in England and Wales who work 32 hours or more per week must complete a minimum of 16 hours of CPD per year (requirements are reduced for solicitors and RELs who work on a part-time basis).

CPD is based on the principles of simplicity and flexibility:

1. The lawyer assumes responsibility for their own development, analyzing their own training and development needs.

2. When they have identified their own training and development needs, they can identify the activities that are likely to meet them.

3. They must record all training and development activities in

their individual training record. The record provides proof against any inspection required and as evidence of CPD credits claimed.

If a solicitor does not comply with CPD requirements, they could face disciplinary procedures and/or to delays in the issue of a practicing certificate. However, registered foreign lawyers are not subject to SRA CPD requirements, although they may be subject to equivalent requirements in their home jurisdiction.

Here are the nuts and bolts of CPD and answers to the most common questions about the CPD scheme.

The CPD scheme was designed by the Solicitor's Regulation Authority in order to make sure that lawyers were learning and growing professionally even while they are not working. CPD ensures that lawyers continue developing professionally, learning about the profession, learning how to maintain a firm, and many other things that can be really beneficial.

What types of activities qualify for CPD credit?

At least 25 per cent of the CPD requirement must be met by participating in courses that are offered by providers authorized by the SRA and which require attendance for one hour or more.

Relevant courses which qualify

- Face-to-face sessions forming part of a course, including those delivered by an authorized distance-learning provider.

- Structured coaching sessions, delivered face to face, of one hour or more, which have written aims and objectives, are documented showing an outcome, and are accredited under an authorization agreement.

- Structured mentoring sessions involving professional development, of one hour or more, delivered face to face, which have written aims and objectives, are documented showing an outcome, and are accredited under an authorization agreement.

The remaining 75 per cent of the CPD requirement, too, may be met by participating in activities as described above; it may also be met by undertaking other activities, outlined below.

To count towards meeting CPD requirements, the activity should be at an appropriate level and contribute to a solicitor's general professional skill and knowledge.

How is CPD credit claimed?

Attendance at courses - CPD course providers notify delegates of the number of hours of credit allocated and the provider's reference; individual solicitors must enter this information, together with the date and course title, into their personal CPD training record.

Distance learning courses - the name of the course provider, the provider's reference, the course title, the date on which the course was undertaken, and the number of hours of credit should be entered into the training record.

If a lawyer delivers delivery/preparation of courses, coaching/ mentoring, writing books/articles and research. Details of the activity and the number of hours undertaken should be entered on the training record. It is advisable to enter in your personal record details of all developmental activities, even if you are unsure whether they can be claimed for CPD credit.

How is the CPD year calculated?

A solicitor's or a registered European lawyer (REL)'s first full CPD year begins on 1 November immediately subsequent to his or her date of admission or registration. Solicitors and RELs admitted or registered on 1 November immediately enter their first CPD year.

CPD is essential to a lawyer's professional work and by using the previous set of questions, criteria, and guideline descriptors; you can really see the importance of CPD in a lawyer's professional life.

Once you become accredited, providing these services will be really beneficial to both you and your client.

Why Become Accredited?

Accreditation means recognition. Coaching isn't yet regarded as a "true" profession at the moment, you need to be ahead of the curve and realize that it soon will be.

Being accredited by the Law Society & the Bar Council to provide CPD will mean:

that lawyers will be sure that you provide what they're looking for

- that lawyers can claim guaranteed CPD credits

- that you are a trusted source of learning

- that you are visible by being listed as an accredited coach/ consultant by the Law Society & the Bar Council

- that you are credible because of the listing , one that doesn't cost you a dime

- that your perfect target market demographic can find you on the list of accredited, therefore approved, suppliers to the legal business (and way ahead of those not accredited)

- that time-poor lawyers seeking CPD accredited coaches will choose the easy route and turn to specialist lists and websites that provide the names of coaches and services they need

- that the younger lawyer demographic, more familiar with

technology, will choose to use websites to find coaches/ trainers - young, impressed clients can become clients for life.

And, while this may seem like a trivial matter, maintaining several steady clients over the long run provides a great deal more security to your business and lifestyle than random sporadic clients at intervals. Delivering solutions to your lawyer clients and being their confident, enables you to achieve just this scenario.

Now you can see why accreditation is a vital step in becoming a coach to legal professionals; boosting your business through creditability and easy marketing directly to your chosen segment.

Solicitor's Management Course

Solicitors (but not RELs) in legal practice or employment in England and Wales are required to attend the Solicitors Regulation Authority Management Course Stage 1 before the end of their third CPD year.

The compulsory Management Course Stage 1 comprises a minimum of seven hours of course attendance. At least three of the following topics must be covered: Managing finance; managing the firm; managing client relations; Managing information and Managing people.

Management Course Stage 2 is optional but many solicitors who wish to become Partners or start their own business opt to take this or other similar management courses.

Structuring CPD Credit Activities

English Solicitors and RELs are encouraged to adopt a planned approach to their CPD; this is a good practice all lawyers and attorneys ought to adopt.

In large firms, career planning usually takes place during the lawyer's yearly appraisal. The lawyer is then encouraged to assess their own individual training needs and link them to the objectives of the organization in which they work. With this clear action plan, both the firm and the lawyer gain greatest benefit from CPD.

How You Can Bring Benefit

You can become accredited to provide CPD training to lawyers. Mentoring and coaching sessions with accredited coaches gain CPD credits. This may seem like a complicated process but it is worth applying as this makes you more attractive to the barrister. They consider that if you have been endorsed by their regulator they you are worth engaging.

Providing CPD courses and coaching to the Bar

Barristers are regulated by the Bar Standards Board which also regulates training providers. You can apply to become a registered provider of CPD accredited courses. The forms can be downloaded from the Bar Standards Board's website. To apply, you need to provide the following information:

- Provide a brief descriptions and synopsis that give a flavor of both the content and the learning experience of the training delivered.

- Describe the rationale, aims and objectives of the course which describe the aims of the training (what it is intended to provide for practitioners in general terms) and objectives (the actions that will be undertaken to meet these aims, in principle in measurable terms). This should include a reference to any skills and competencies that the training delivers and assesses.

- Explain for whom the training likely to be most suitable? Describe the level of practitioner is the training most aimed at considering their Year of Call.

- State what the expected outcomes are for the barrister. List what the learning outcomes are for the practitioner.

- Describe the Teaching Strategies and Resources which will be utilized. These should describe how the expected outcomes will be achieved and through the training/learning styles adopted. Provide a brief explanation of the intended resources and facilities available to practitioners undertaking this course.

- Explain whether the attainment of outcomes is assessed in any way or how practitioners will be able to demonstrate the expected outcomes learnt from the training.

- Specify the type of training and format that will be delivered. Distance learning including online courses, Webinars (seminars streamed live via a website), recorded seminars/lectures/training sessions for DVD distribution count towards CPD points.

Determine your client's training by completing a Training Needs Analysis (TNA). This can include a strengths, weaknesses, opportunities, threats (SWOT) analysis, based on their own profile and circumstances to help them gauge their needs.

Knowing their needs will enable your client to identify the types of training they should undertake, for inclusion in their own training and development plan, which can include buying your services.

This is a win-win scenario - your client completes their CPD requirements effectively whilst getting their needs met; you get a satisfied and empowered customer.

Invest in your own Continuing Development

I'm probably preaching to the converted but I'll go ahead anyway. It is beneficial for you to invest in your own development. Ensure that your clients pay you what you are worth so that you don't have to work all the time and you can focus on your development and that of your business so that you can serve them better.

Keep innovating

The coaching business is becoming more like a profession. It is currently unregulated or self regulated. It is only a matter of time before it becomes regulated. All businesses go through five cycles.

The first cycle is when a business or an industry is new. This is the early adopters.

The second cycle is one of rapid growth. Coaching went through this phase in the last 10 years. Nowadays it seems like everyone is a coach. But don't worry, that is not the case, it's just because of the people you hang around with. It is the case that anyone can set themselves up as a coach and coaching is now mainstream. However, there are people who are not as professional as others and have given the profession a bad name.

The third stage is regulation. After rapid growth comes the inevitable regulation. Now this could be self regulation or imposed governmental regulation. If the industry does not self regulate then regulation can be imposed by the government.

The fourth stage is amalgamation. This is where the big players come in and dominate the market. This has been happening coaching in the last few years.

The fifth stage will be the stage of innovation. This is where new and creative ideas come through. As coaches we can keep innovating and moving the industry forward.

Have a laugh

Lawyer: "Did you tell your lawyer that your husband had offered you indignities?"

Witness: "He didn't offer me nothin'". He just said I could have the furniture."

and another...

Lawyer: "Do you drink when you're on duty?"

Witness: "I don't drink when I'm on duty, unless I come on duty drunk."

Help me if you can

- Learn to manage my profits

- Manage my personal finances

- Financial management

- Financial planning

- Manage my business' finances

- Get investment to start my own practice

- Get investment to expand my firm

- Succession planning

- Manage my accounts and reporting

- Financial planning before I start a family

Now do something!
Knowledge is potential power.
Action is real power!

What 3 actions could you take right now?

1. _____

   _____

   _____

2. _____

   _____

   _____

3. _____

   _____

   _____

Chapter 19 - Handle With Care - Deliver a Gold Standard Service

Whilst most lawyers have problems adapting to the ever changing market, they must feel comfortable with the speed of adopting their own changes. They face a whole bunch of new decisions - how to include marketing and sales; how to choose which processes they are comfortable with; how they will feel and deal with what they adopt.

In working with lawyers it is essential they feel that they are being treated as an equal; they are fellow professionals, just in a different field to yours. Build your relationship with your lawyer client through a mutual respect gained from truly being interested in them: ask them about their life, how they work, what they feel they are weak at, what they feel their strong points are. Make sure that you get to know them before you start making assumptions based on the general state of the legal business and what you perceive their work involves.

Building an honest, caring relationship with integrity, means your client knows where they stand.

Get insurance

This is just good business practice and you know it makes sense. Compared to the level of insurance lawyers are required to have and how much they have to pay for it what coaches are required to pay is a lot less! State in your client care letter that you have insurance.

Send a Client Information Letter

Attorneys, solicitors and lawyers are accustomed to sending out client care letters. In fact they are obliged under their

Code of Conduct to do so. If you also send a letter then you are demonstrating a level of professionalism not generally seen amongst coaches.

EXAMPLE CLIENT INFORMATION LETTER

Dear John

Coaching you to Success

Thank you for engaging me to work with you in assisting you to achieve your goal of reaching your business targets. .

I confirm your first coaching session will take place on Monday 21 March 2011 at 5pm at your Chambers.

I have agreed to provide you with the following services:

State the services you will provide

If you require my assistance with any other matters please contact me.

My contact details are:

Telephone (land line)

Telephone (cell/mobile)

Email

My normal office hours are 9.30am to 5.30pm.

When I am out of the office, please leave a message with Kelly my personal assistant, who will ensure that your message is passed promptly to me.

I have a message answering service to take any messages you may wish to leave outside of my office hours.

We respond to messages within 24 hours at the latest and usually more quickly.

If you leave a message, to ensure that we can reply promptly and efficiently, we should be grateful if you would leave your name, your contact number, times at which you are available to be contacted and details of your query or message.

In the event of any concerns that you may have about our service to you, please let me know, so that the matter can be resolved.

Fees

I also enclose my initial invoice for £6,000 in respect of the first six coaching sessions. Please note that invoices are payable before the commencement of our services.

Payment can be made either by check or by bank transfer. Please allow 3 to 4 working days for the banks to deal with the transfer.

Complaints policy

We hope you won't need it but we have a complaints policy in place.

We will send you a coaching agreement/ we enclose two copies of our coaching agreement. Please sign and return one copy/ or please sign and give one copy to your coach when she arrives.

I look forward to helping you achieve your goals!

Enc: Invoice

Have a Written Coaching Agreement

I always use a written coaching agreement to set out the mutual expectations on the coach and the coachee. It is not written as a formal contract that lawyers are used to drafting. The agreement client care letters and documents are available on our website. See the Resources page for information.

There are two types of people in the world. Both are blessed to enter a wide open grand green field of opportunity under which lie vast treasures.

One person looks around the field grabs any shovel they can and begins digging a hole in the ground looking for gold. When this person gets a few shovels deep they discover either:

A. they are not hitting gold as fast as they thought they would or

B. there is not as much gold as they thought.

They stop digging and move on to another random point in the field. They grab a new fancy tool or shovel and they dig again looking for gold. Again they find disappointment so they move on and on and on.

At the end of this person's life their field of opportunity looks like a bunch of half dug holes.

The other person however approaches the field of opportunity differently. They scan their horizon and decide where they would like to stake their claim in life. They too begin digging down doing looking for gold. They too may quickly discover either

A. they are not hitting gold as fast as they thought they would

B. there is not as much gold as they thought

But this is where their fate unfolds differently than their unfocussed peers. They keep digging. They think to themselves:

There is some gold here. Maybe not as much as I thought as early on as I thought but there is gold. They keep digging. Working hard. Staying focused. But soon enough they hit the big pay day. That vein of gold that is more abundant and awe-inspiring than they ever imagined. They set up fencepost of fortune. Then they move to another spot aligned with their previous success. They set a fencepost there. At the end of this person's life their field of opportunity line looks like a long line of strong foundations stretching into the sunset.

A life of dabbling leads to failure. While a life of mastery leads to wealth. It's tempting to try and be everything to everyone. Don't try to be everything under the sun. You can't know everything and do everything.

You will be more successful if you focus on one opportunity at a time. So dig deep and you will create foundations. Understand the value of hard work. Don't be put off by the hard work that might be required. Put in the time to develop your business and yourself. It may take blood sweat and tears to mine this new opportunity but don't give up. Master your craft, whatever it is. Work towards a life of mastery as this will lead to a life of meaning. If you emphasize mastery this will encourage you to build a successful business built on hard work and dedication which will stand the test of time.

Have a laugh

Lawyer: "What is your relationship with the plaintiff?"
Witness: "She is my daughter."
Lawyer: "Was she your daughter on February 22, 1985?"

and another...

A guy walks into a post office one day to see a middle-aged, balding man standing at the counter methodically placing "Love" stamps on bright pink envelopes with hearts all over them.

He then takes out a perfume bottle and starts spraying scent all over them. His curiosity getting the better of him, he goes up to the balding man and asks him what he is doing.

The man says "I'm sending out 1,000 Valentine cards signed, 'Guess who?'"

"But why?" asks the man.

"I'm a divorce lawyer."

Help me If You Can

- Participate in the community
- Find synergistic projects to partner with
- Raise my profile as a giving firm

Environment

- Feng shui my office and home
- Introduce energy saving products
- Meet carbon emission targets
- De clutter

Healing relationships

- Communication with my significant other

Chapter 20 - Legal Business in 2020

Dramatic shifts are predicted for the legal profession by 2020. Research conducted recently by Emergent Research predicts 20 key demographic, social, economic and technology trends that will change the world over the next decade highlights opportunities for small business growth. This includes the growth in small lawyer businesses. One of the primary problems legal business owners have is with getting things done. A coach can hold people accountable. You can help them to create well formed outcomes, set goals and achieve their goals. This 8-year look into the future predicts the global economy will swell with the addition of one billion new middle-class consumers. Health and wellness will become top-of-wallet issues for the world's consumers and cloud computing will begin to erode the foundation of traditional bricks-and-mortar commerce. In short, brace yourself for world-changing tectonic shifts.

"We are already seeing fundamental shifts that are changing the way we all live and operate, but rarely do you see so many trends directly affecting the global economy and community in such a short time," Kris Halvorsen, Intuit's chief innovation officer, said in a statement.

While trend-spotting can often be as chancy an occupation as reading tea leaves, here are the top four substantive bread-and-butter economic issues that the report identified:

What this all Means for Lawyers

Lawyers will have to embrace and use technology to survive to meet people where they are. This means that if customers are technology-savvy and using mobile social services, then learning about these services and, how they may work for your business, is essential. As convenience continues to move up in priority for many, technology is the glue that can help to identify, reach and transact with new customers or hold on to your current ones.

Additionally, partnerships with other local businesses may help expand your markets. Partners can deliver fresh and relevant data for you to consider about what your customers are seeking and how best to deliver something that they would find irresistible. I've seen food companies paring a special selection with an entertainment venue, or using farmer's markets or pop-up shops to get in front of new prospects quickly and affordably. These are tools available today that give business owners the chance to engage with their customers and FOC (friends of customers) in memorable ways. The goals here are to: (a) learn from the experiment or trial; (b) create buzz and delight those who have newly found you, and (c) decide if your business should expand by incorporating this new type of offer going forward.

Have the last laugh

This is a call to an IT support centre from someone in a law firm

"Good Afternoon, may I help you?"

"Yes, well, I'm having trouble with my computer."

"What sort of trouble?"

"Well, I was just typing along, and all of a sudden the words went away."

"Went away?" "They disappeared."

"Hmm. So what does your screen look like now?"

"Nothing."

"Nothing?"

"It's blank; it won't accept anything when I type."

"Are you still in the screen, or did you get

out?"

"How do I tell?"

"Can you see the C: prompt on the screen?"

"What's a sea-prompt?"

"Never mind. Can you move the cursor around on the screen?"

"There isn't any cursor: I told you, it won't accept anything I type."

"Does your monitor have a power indicator?"

"What's a monitor?"

"It's the thing with the screen on it that looks like a TV. Does it have a little light that tells you when it's on?"

"I don't know."

"Well, then look on the back of the monitor and find where the power cord goes into it. Can you see that?"

"Yes, I think so."

"Great. Follow the cord to the plug, and tell me if it's plugged into the wall."

"... Yes, it is."

"When you were behind the monitor, did you notice that there were two cables plugged into the back of it, not just one?"

"No."

"Well, there are. I need you to look back there again and find the other cable."

"... Okay, here it is."

"Follow it for me, and tell me if it's plugged securely into the back of your computer."

"I can't reach."

"Uh huh. Well, can you see if it is?"

"No."

"Even if you maybe put your knee on something and lean way over?"

"Oh, it's not because I don't have the right angle - it's because it's dark."

"Dark?"

"Yes - the office light is off, and the only light I have is coming in from the window."

"Well, turn on the office light then."

"I can't."

"No? Why not?"

"Because there's a power cut"

"A power... A power cut? Aha, Okay, we've got it licked now. Do you still have the boxes and manuals and packing stuff your computer came in?"

"Well, yes, I keep them in the closet."

"Good. Go get them, and unplug your system and pack it up just like it was when you got it. Then take it back to the store you bought it from."

"Really? Is it that bad?"

"Yes, I'm afraid it is."

"Well, all right then, I suppose. What do I tell them?"

"Tell them you're too stupid to own a computer."

This employee was allegedly dismissed and has sued for unfair dismissal!

Thank you for taking the time to read this book. Now it's up to you what you do with the information!

It's up to me

I get discouraged now and then
When there are clouds so gray,
Until I think about the things
That happened yesterday.
I do not mean the day before
Or those of months ago,
But all the yesterdays in which
I had the chance to grow.
I think of opportunities
That I allowed to die,
And those I took advantage of
Before they passed me by.
And I remember that the past
Presented quite a plight,
But somehow I endured it and,
The future seemed all right.
And I remind myself that I
Am capable and free
And my success and happiness
Are really up to me.

James J. Metcalfe

PROGRAMS AND PRODUCTS FOR COACHES
CONSULTANTS AND TRAINERS

The How to Sell to Lawyers™ System

Are you ready to cash in on the gold in your mind and the legal market for coaching, training and consulting?

This program gives you the COMPLETE, PROVEN SYSTEM for using the potential you have locked inside you to achieve financial goals. The How to Sell to Lawyers System will open your eyes to the deep reservoirs of gold that exists.

The How to Sell to Lawyers TM System contains the complete plan for developing this new market. Here's just some of what you'll learn on this life changing program:

- How to have well paying clients knocking down your door

- Why you are getting the negative responses you are getting from lawyers - and how to massively improve that result

- How to overcome objections easily, effortlessly, and elegantly and have fun doing it!

- How to have 80% of your business come from referrals

- How to have your legal clients give you referrals without you even asking

- How to treble your fees and really get paid what you are worth and still be in integrity with your purpose

What you will receive:

Includes the complete CD set presented in 30 minute segments for your learning pleasure and convenience and your Personal Workbook.

Free Legal Gold™ Webinars - nuggets to win more business and to dig for the motherlode. www.howtoselltolawyers.com

Legal Gold™ Seminars - Finding the hidden treasure in the legal market. A fun and interactive game inspired seminar with hands on learning.

Midas Touch Consulting™ - One to one consulting to guarantee you'll win a contract with a law firm - Lending you the Midas Touch.

Let's Coach the Lawyers System™ - Two days complete System for coaching lawyers. Includes the bespoke Bar2Bench™; Fast Track to Silk™; Partnership Track™ Technologies.

Lawdacity Coaching Academy™ - a bespoke coaching program for those who want to become accredited to coach lawyers. We will apply for accreditation by the Law Society of England and Wales, the Bar Council and the International Coaching Federation. Includes 2 days on the Elegant Marketing and Elegant Enrolment technologies.

International Legal Gold™ Mastermind Groups - Exclusive Support Groups for Lawdacity Accredited coaches in the legal profession.

PROGRAMS AND PRODUCTS FOR LAWYERS

Legal Gold for Lawyers

My next book informing lawyers of the benefits of coaching and introducing them to coaching and specific coaching programs for barristers, solicitors and attorneys who want to become judges or partners in their firms.

Bar2Bench™

A bespoke program for solicitors and barristers who want to become judges.

This program will cover the following

The five competencies which you must achieve

Detailed guidance on the career track to follow if you want to go down this route

How to prepare for the examination

How to prepare thoroughly for the role play where you will be the judge

How to prepare for the interview

Information for you on how to work with your assessors so they can provide the best possible assessment of your performance

Includes a special report on the assessment process

Partnership Track™

A bespoke program for solicitors and attorneys who want to become Partners in big firms.

Includes

Deciding and setting SMART goals

Values

Mentoring

Profiling

Fast Track to Silk™

A bespoke program for barristers and solicitor advocates who want to go down the road of applying to be Queens Counsel one day.

It includes

Early career planning

The six competencies that you must master to an excellent standard to be considered

How to demonstrate your competency in

Understanding and using the law

Written Advocacy

Oral Advocacy

Working together - Leadership and management

Diversity

Integrity

Guidance on how to really complete the 64 page application form

Also includes detailed information for assessors

A model completed assessment

How to prepare so you have a fun and easy interview instead of a "grilling"

Legally Bold™

In this book I will set out my ideas for transforming the way we practice law in the UK.

If you are a lawyer wanting a more successful career and life go to www.LawyersSuccessCoach.com to find out how we can assist you.

Giving back -

Lawdacity is a lifetime member of Buy1Give1.

Every time you buy one of our programs 10 per cent of the revenue goes to funding training and development for entrepreneurs in Africa and India or to help people in the UK who are being sued or are having their properties repossessed (foreclosure) and can't afford to pay a lawyer.

Raise the Bar™

Coaching/ Consulting Program

If I chose you to work with me …

in a Consulting/ Coaching Program for an entire year - focusing on multiplying your income, how much more do you think you could make over the next 12 months?

Email me at

Coaching@CarolineNewman.com

For more information see my website

www.CarolineNewman.com

"I always have many projects on the go and needed a good coach to help sort through them and prioritize. I was having a very hard time determining what my first steps should be. After working with Caroline and strategizing about my situation and what my business goals were, she was able to help me set my priorities and take immediate action. Her ability to cut through the fog was invaluable in helping me get clear on my marketing message."

Daniel Browne, Former Investment Banker, Deutsche Bank, Energy Expert and Author

.......wait, there's more! Coming Soon!

Lawnch and Grow™

A comprehensive coaching and consulting program for lawyers who want to set up their own law firm or for Barristers who have Direct Access to clients.

PLAW™- Progressive Lawyers Association Worldwide (working title)

A membership-based on line association for lawyers and attorneys who are progressive and want to move the legal profession forward.

UPLAW™ - University for Progressive Lawyers Around the World (working title)

An on-line and off line centre of learning for lawyers, attorneys and judges providing personal and professional development courses. The courses will cover the matters raised in this book as well as collaboration, coaching and mediation as alternatives to litigation.

Lawdacity™ Law School for non-lawyers

We believe that law should not be the preserve of lawyers and that everyone should know their basic rights. We will provide courses for people who want to know their legal rights and responsibilities. We will also provide information for business people on the basic knowledge they need to have in running their businesses. The courses for businesses will be very practical and will include:

Employment Law: Hiring and Firing; Diversity and equality; Disabled workers and reasonable adjustments; Health and safety

Business contracts: Setting up a company; Setting up a Social Enterprise; Shareholders agreements; Set up your business so it can be sold - if that is your exit strategy; Selling your business; ..... and much much more

Other Courses and Programs

Networking for Success - how to become a more effective and confident business networker

Business Networking Public Seminars - Lawdacity™ hold a nationwide program of public seminars. Presentation Skills and Advanced Presentation Skills

Networking for Women Only!

Business Networking Web Seminars

In-house Lawyers business networking training

LinkedIn Training: available as an in-house workshop, public seminar, or web seminar.

You will find the Lawdacity™ website your ideal resource for examples of training profiles, training needs analyses, and training and development plans. You will also find completed examples and blank forms. (Lawyers are very busy, especially those who are sole practitioners or in small partnerships without dedicated Human Resources support, would appreciate your helping them with these).

No Court Solutions

This Community Interest company (Social Enterprise) will provide training and help for people in England and Wales who can't afford a lawyer or who are being sued or may need to take their case to a court. Our aim is to encourage mediation and alternative dispute resolution as a *Re-Solution* to any conflict or disagreement which might otherwise end up in court.

FROM THE DESK OF

Caroline has an LLB (Listening, Loving and Being) from the University of Life. She also graduated with a master's degree in law from London School of Economics (University of London) and an honors degree in law from University of Westminster (London). She is a certified Neuro Linguistic Practitioner Trainer and Master Practitioner. She is a certified Master Practitioner in Timeline Therapy™. She is a licensed

Life Success Consultant and highly trained and experienced Professional Speaker. Healing therapies include Hypnotherapy and Theta Healing (used only as required). She is a lifelong learner.

Following a successful career which included senior positions in local government and the charity sector, Caroline became an English solicitor in 2001 with SJ Berwin LLP (a top City of London and European law firm). She also set up her own successful law practice. She has been coaching and consulting attorneys, barristers, solicitors and judges who want more success in their lives and helping them reach their goals since 2004. She has sold and delivered training, consulting and coaching services to barristers' chambers, law firms, local authorities and central government since 2003. She has also trained the police and members of the armed forces. She has worked with over 4000 lawyers in that time.

She was an elected member of the Council of the Law Society of England and Wales for six years, chair of its Diversity

Committee and member of its Management Board.

Caroline was given an award for Services to the Legal Profession in 2008 and invited to the Queen' Garden Party at Buckingham Palace.

Companies, Law Firms and Bar Associations: If you have a conference or staff development weekend and want a motivating, lively speaker Caroline can deliver for you! She can speak on the following topics:

- Effective and fun business networking

- Building Successful Teams

- Going for Legal Gold™ - How to Sell so Lawyers will Buy

- Leadership

- Giant Leap to Success™- Caroline's personal story which will move and delight your audience

- She can tailor any of these topics for your business or organization.

Follow Caroline at:

Caroline's blog: www.carolinenewman.com/blog

Twitter: carolinewnewman1

Facebook: www.facebook.com/CarolineNewman

YouTube: CarolineNewmanLaw

Linkedin

Skype: CarolineNewman1

What others are saying about Caroline Newman and Legal Gold

Are you looking for answers to questions like "how can I grow my coaching business?" or "what direction should I take?" or "what's the best and most effective step I should take now to accelerate my consulting business?" This book will give you the answers. Look no further. All you have to do is read this book and you will see and feel a brighter future for yourself and for your business. By the time you finish reading this book you will feel a shift and a certain mental clarity. For those with cloudy priorities, this will certainly give you clear guidance as to how to start. For those who had their priorities straight already, it will help you get there faster and give you the treasure map you need to take your business to the next level by tapping into a new market".

Andy Harrington - International Professional Speaker and Trainer, Power to Achieve

In your hands is an interesting book: it's about lawyers and how you can build mutually rewarding partnerships with them. In this way, the book is unique for it connects lawyers to being human with needs to specialists who can provide for them. Caroline has placed her heart and soul into this bridge - read it, use it and create success for all parties involved.

Benn Abdy-Collins, Transitions Mentor & Holistic Practitioner, Specialist in Dealing with Times of Personal Change

I always have many projects on the go and needed a good coach to help sort through them and prioritize. I was having a very hard time determining what my first steps should be. After working with Caroline and strategizing about my situation and what my business goals were, she was able to help me set my priorities and take immediate action. Her ability to cut through the fog was invaluable in helping me get clear on my marketing message. "

Daniel Browne, Former Investment Banker, Deutsche Bank, Author

This book is a great resource for Coaches and Trainers looking to expand into a new and potentially exciting and lucrative market. It is packed full of practical tips, ideas and useable nuggets of information that the reader can put into action straightaway. You will also gain an overview of the legal profession which gives you the confidence to go forth and mine for that legal gold!

Marilyn Devonish Co-Author of Stories of Transformation, Founder of TranceFormations™.com, Certified Life & Executive Coach

"Legal Gold is an inspiring, easy read on how to actually MAKE money from your attorney. Caroline Newman has created an innovative approach to partnering in a WIN/WIN situation that is new and fascinating! I give this book "two thumbs up" for exposing a goldmine of information that will fill your coffers".

Linda Forsythe Founder, Mentors Magazine

For more testimonials and information visit my websites:

www.CarolineNewman.com

www.LawyersSuccessCoach.com

2045993R00118

Printed in Great Britain
by Amazon.co.uk, Ltd.,
Marston Gate.